INTERNATIONAL HOTEL AND CATERING
MANAGEMENT CONSULTANT

Alfred Motson F.H.C.I.M.A., F.C.F.A.
34 BADINGHAM DRIVE, FETCHAM PARK,
SURREY KT22 9EU
TEL: LEATHERHEAD (53) 75146

HOW TO SELL BANQUETS

How to Sell Banquets

The Key to Conference and Function Promotion

Derek Taylor
MA(Cantab), FHCIMA

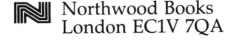
Northwood Books
London EC1V 7QA

Published 1979

© Northwood Publications Ltd and Derek Taylor,
1979

ISBN 7198 2734 5

ACKNOWLEDGEMENT
The author wishes to acknowledge, with many
thanks, the assistance of David Bloomfield of Adam
& Bloomfield, 152 Shaftesbury Avenue, London
WC2, who designed the letterhead for the fictional
King William Hotel used in the text.

A 'Catering Times' book

Printed and bound in Great Britain by
Eyre & Spottiswoode Ltd, Thanet Press, Margate,
Kent.

Contents

For both Mothers

For many years now I have had a quotation from Cecil King hanging over my desk as a dreadful warning. It reads:

> 'Many sectors of British top management are afraid to change, failing to give leadership, and eternally seeking compromise and a quiet life.'

That was said in 1965 and it is still true. Perhaps it will always be, but in banqueting the winds of change are blowing hard. This book is about those changes.

Introduction

Back in 1964, when I wrote *Hotel and Catering Sales Promotion*, it seemed appropriate to start with a chapter entitled, 'Is Selling Respectable?' The answer for the majority of the industry at that time would have been a resounding 'no'. Selling and salesmen were looked down upon by some, partly because – as their opponents saw it – they lowered the tone of the industry. There was also a criticism – seldom voiced – that the salesman, by his very presence, brought into question the part the manager had to play in the area of sales promotion. Was the manager to be a salesman, too? Most managers would have wished to answer 'no' to that question as well, not only because they considered selling to be a low-status occupation, but also because it made considerable demands on their courage.

One has to admit that all salesmen have pangs of nervousness at first, so it is easy to see how daunting many managers must have found the prospect. But with time and experience, almost all salesmen find the initial uneasiness disappears, largely because the great majority of customers are pleasant and understanding. They are prepared to accept the interruption of someone breaking into their day's work and asking for business as a matter of course: which it is. And for my own part, in twenty years of selling, I cannot recall more than a dozen or so customers who were rude or unreasonable.

At the time I wrote that book, not much more than a decade ago, managers who had not been trained to sell the facilities they could offer, were quick to resist the suggestion of this new demand on their time and ability. They held to the popular image of the typical salesman as a fast-talking, cheap, not too honest, semi-confidence trickster. The expression 'touting for business', never said in a complimentary way, came readily to the lips. Not the kind of person any self-respecting manager wanted to be!

The difference between the American and the British attitude to selling was summed up, for me, in two separate instances on television. In America a newly-elected candidate for the Presidency, being interviewed on coast-to-coast TV, was asked how he hoped to defeat the incumbent President. 'Well, I hope I am a better salesman than he is,' he answered. This, presumably, was exactly the sort of reply the majority of Americans expected from a candidate for the highest office in the land. At about the same time in Britain, Harold Wilson, as he then was, the Prime Minister, was explaining a new policy to the nation. In a depressing tone he told his television audience, 'I don't want you to feel that I'm trying to put this idea over like some super salesman'. And again, presumably the phraseology was appropriate to the nation's attitude to selling.

Whether the British in general have moved very far from the viewpoint of those days is not too easy to decide. This book is for those who *have* adopted a different posture; who recognise that there is precious little point in manufacturing a product, or offering a service, if you don't make enough effort to sell it.

The number of professional salesmen in the industry has increased by leaps and bounds since the early 1960s, when the Hotel Sales Managers' Association was founded by half-a-dozen of us – and of those eager pioneers, a couple were scarcely members of the hotel industry at all! Happily, since then, there have been a great many enthusiastic newcomers; the vast majority of them young, a great many of them highly intelligent; and a now increasing number of them are women. Frankly, it doesn't make any difference at all whether a good salesperson is male or female, attractive or not. What does matter is that they be intelligent, because selling is a thinking profession.

This book deals primarily with banqueting sales; but banqueting is a microcosm of all sales. If we concentrate our attention on sales techniques in this area of the industry, it will provide us with valuable information on how to sell in the other departments too. In addition, banqueting is the one area in the hotel industry where selling has been traditionally accepted. The Banqueting Manager has always been expected to have lengthier contact than any other employee with the client in order to reach agreement on the many details to be settled. On occasions, it has been uphill work for the client rather than the salesman. I have known cases, in a few hotels in the bad old days, when banqueting managers needed more than a little persuading to accept bookings on 'inconvenient' days – Sundays and public holidays were never popular with them for large functions – and from clients whose business they considered 'beneath' their establishment.

Banqueting managers who adopt these attitudes (if there are still any about) should not hold their jobs at all. And neither I nor anyone else can help them. This book is for those who want to *succeed*.

What is selling? It is not a magic formula. It is the absorption of knowledge from a variety of experienced people around you; and putting the knowledge into practice.

I was helped by so many people that it is impossible to name them all. I can only hope that my expressions of gratitude in the past have made each and every one of them aware of the part they have played in the assimilation of the material for this book.

Perhaps the greatest lesson any salesman can learn is that you can never stop learning. The knowledge you need is there to be absorbed all the time. I remember going on a sales call with my good friend, Ron de Young (London and Continental Advertising) when he was a salesman with me. His market research started the moment he saw the lift man, and by the time we had reached the floor we wanted, he had already identified the organiser of the firm's annual staff party. And the example of a young salesman, Bob Davis, whose attention to detail in looking after clients was such that one American, in admiration, asked, 'Can I go to the loo by myself!' Or Jimmy Horner, a great banqueting manager, who taught me never to be overawed by the importance of a client's title; that everyone was human and everyone was a valuable client. Then there were Peter Kubicek and Andrei Edington, who believed in creative banqueting; Albert Stratta, whose standards of presentation would have graced the Trooping of the Colour; and innumerable clients who taught me what they wanted. I learned something from them all.

Amongst the books which I found helpful were Vance Packard's *Hidden Persuaders*; Coffman's *Profits through Promotion*; Jerry della Femina's *From Those Wonderful Folk Who Gave You Pearl Harbour*; and Heinz Goldman's *How to Win Customers*. It is not a very large bibliography because I did not learn much of my trade from books. I learned from sitting at the feet of good salesmen, just listening and learning. I valued the help, in the early days, of salesmen outside the industry too; people like Peter Pratt (TWA), Merv Elliott (Playtex), Dick Hurst (Hudson & Knight), Jack Bocier (Unilever), and of course Keith Barry, who taught me how to write, and John Tanfield, who taught me how to think. If you find that this book helps you with your selling problems, I shall have the added satisfaction of repaying my own teachers for their hard work.

1
What Matters

Most hotels produce a list of the banquets they are looking after about a week before the events take place. These lists give the numbers of guests to be served, the rooms to be used, the way the tables are to be set up, and much other information. What such lists seldom convey is any indication of the importance of the function to the client. To the hotel the occasion normally seems just another dinner; another group of guests to be fed, seated, amused or instructed. To the client it is a very different matter.

For the mother of the bride, the wedding is the event of a lifetime, with no detail too trivial for her careful consideration. For the Sales Director, the occasion might represent the only time in the year when his Managing Director sees the whole sales force on parade; and the Sales Director wants to make a good impression. For the organiser of a retirement dinner, it is the one chance a group of colleagues will have to honour an esteemed and popular member of their group at the end of his business career. For the charity ball committee, it is the culmination of all their efforts to raise money in a good cause.

I learned this lesson about the difference in attitude between the hotel staff and the client many years ago when British European Airways, as they were then, had booked some dinners at the Washington Hotel. Many of the functions were to celebrate inaugural flights, when the airline would bring press and distinguished visitors from a European city to which it was flying for the first time. So I suggested ways of theming the dinners to bring out the airline's Anglo-French or Anglo-German accord. One of the dinners did not fall into this pattern of inaugural celebrations and, as nobody asked for any particular theme, a perfectly average sort of menu was served. It was only on the night that we discovered that the dinner was to mark the retirement of a distinguished travel writer. At the end of the evening, one of the managers said to the client, 'I wish we'd known it was an important occasion. We could have produced something special'. To which the client, quite rightly, replied, 'All my dinners are special!'

So they are, but in most hotels not enough importance is given to this crucial fact. Sometimes, as you will see, points which are of the utmost importance to the client may appear quite minor and inconsequential to the management. This is because not enough attention is given to one of the fundamental rules in selling – always put yourself in the place of the client. If *you* were booking the function, what would be important to *you*? What would *you* be trying to achieve? What would make *you* decide against one hotel in favour of another? What combination of factors would make up your mind and finally encourage you to place the order?

Conferences

Conferences are an increasingly important part of hotel business. For the purposes of this discussion, they may be divided into the following categories:
  1. Company conferences.
  2. Association meetings.
  3. Courses produced by consultants.
  4. Amateur conferences.

Company Conferences: The company conference organiser is usually the easiest type of client to deal with in this field of business. He will most probably have had some previous experience at arranging and negotiating for this type of function, and will therefore know exactly what he wants. When he says that something will happen, you can usually rely on his word. Normally either he himself or his immediate superior will decide where the business is to be placed.

To the company organiser the following specific points are important:

1. The speed and efficiency of breakfast service: If company staff are staying in the hotel on the night before the conference, this is vital. Nothing annoys the opening speaker – who is usually the most senior person at the meeting – more than the late arrival of delegates muttering excuses about the long delays in the service of breakfast. I have moved many major conferences out of their existing hotels by emphasising the reliability and speed of the breakfast service – something that takes place before the conference even starts.

2. The quietness of the conference room: You cannot run a successful conference with kitchen or vacuum cleaner noises drowning the speaker, with dustbins rattling or the clatter of staff laying up for lunch within earshot. It is vital that the conference room should be free of all disturbances of this kind.

3. The seclusion of the hotel: If your hotel is secluded or has only one exit at

night, this can be a key selling factor when you are trying to get the business of a conference. Make it clear to the company manager that you understand his problems and point out to him either that your hotel is too far from the bright lights to make late-night excursions worth the delegates' while; or that he would be able to position himself strategically near the single exit and discourage such forays. Even if he has already actually given up hope of keeping his charges within the hotel bounds, it shows that you appreciate his difficulties and realise that delegates who get to bed at four in the morning are unlikely to be assimilating vital facts at five o'clock that same afternoon! This kind of rapport is vital in creating the correct relationship between client and management.

It goes without saying that the client will also want to know that the conference room is large enough for his requirements, that the price will not go beyond his budget, and that the food will be eatable. These points apply to every client. But it is the extra ones I have mentioned: swift breakfast service, a quiet conference room, and the seclusion of the hotel, that are of special importance to the company conference organiser.

Association Meetings: We refer here to the smaller associations and clubs. Larger gatherings of such organisations are dealt with under the heading of Amateur Conferences. The salesman's first job is to establish who in the association is the decision maker. It might be the association secretary, the man you are most likely to be dealing with, particularly when he is an experienced, respected and powerful character. However, it might be the chairman, who has his own preferences and to whom the secretary may act as a loyal servant. Sometimes it might be a third member who just happens to be the power behind the scenes because he provides the money, has the largest number of votes, knows more about everything, or is simply the strongest character at the meetings. The salesman has to identify where the power lies. The best way of doing this is to invite the secretary to bring whichever executives of the association he thinks appropriate to lunch at the hotel in order to see the facilities. When they are all with you, it is not difficult to see who is the dominant character and to whose views the group defers. Having identified the decision maker, concentrate primarily on selling to that man. The others may contribute their opinions, but you will be wise to sell to the decision maker rather than to the group as a whole. Talk to everybody, but concentrate on the decision maker.

Associations, unlike business companies, are not concerned whether members attend their meetings or not, nor are they interested in what they have done the night before. The delegates are free agents and if they choose not to arrive at all when the association's affairs are being discussed, that is their business. Consequently you have to be a little more wary of the numbers you are given for association meetings. They are usually based on the maximum number entitled to attend, rather than the numbers who actually do. Don't ask, therefore, how many people are on the committee, but how many usually attend the meetings.

Consultant Courses: Courses produced by consultants are quite different again. The decision maker is simple to identify because it is his responsibility to set up the course. The question of whether anybody is going to attend is another matter altogether. The consultants can be compared with travel agents arranging package tours; they reserve the space and advertise the package. If nobody buys, they cancel the space. This is quite unlike the position with company or association meetings. Frankly, with a poor consultancy company or an uninteresting subject, the business you are initially offered isn't worth the paper it's written on. The course will be cancelled when nobody buys it, and that cancellation will come as late as the consultants find allowable. They will have spent money on producing brochures for the course or on advertising it, hired lecturers or speakers and used up their own expensive time. They will live in hope that there will be a last-minute flood of business and so by the time the hotel gets the cancellation, the chances of reselling the space are negligible.

Now what is your attitude about cancellation charges? In fairness to consultants, a great many of whom are successful and efficient, a large number of people do attend their courses every year. Those people would not be using hotels if it were not for the efforts of the consultants, who risk their own money to fill the hotel beds and banqueting rooms. Those are not, of course, their objectives; it is just one of the side effects – but none the less valuable to us for that. If we are too hard on consultants, they will go bankrupt or choose a hotel which treats them more kindly. The best attitude to this type of business is to accept it only when there is little likelihood of anything more secure being offered. If that seems rather harsh on a company with a good track record, then by all means look at the record. If the company usually manages to secure an audience, take the rough with the smooth. If a consultant company gives you ten conferences and has to cancel two because of lack of support, you are still eight conferences better off. The biggest selling point to the organiser is how generous you are going to be in letting him off the hook if nobody buys the course, or how you will react if the course he booked for fifty delegates is now to be attended by only ten. Flexibility and co-operation matter more than anything to consultants in this kind of business.

Amateur Conferences: These are the ones where a senior executive of an organisation finds himself, often for the first time in his life, with the responsi-

16

bility of organising a large conference. Take an international conference for example; the British section of, shall we say, The International Cauliflower Growers' Association agrees to host the annual gathering. (If there is such a body, I can only say that any similarity to any other Cauliflower Association, past or present, is purely coincidental!) The Chairman of the Cauliflower Association might be an absolute genius on a ploughed field; but his knowledge of simultaneous translation facilities, the production of technical study papers for delegates, or the handling of registration for one thousand delegates is unlikely to be the reason for his eminence in the association. The organisation of their own national annual meeting might be well within the association's capabilities, but this much larger event almost certainly is not. What the association needs more than anything is expert guidance.

This is where the hotel can sell itself hard to secure the business. A hotel that might come about fourth in the market place in terms of quality and value can still walk off with the business if it can offer this kind of expertise. Convince the Chairman that you know all there is to know about what it takes to make the event a success in every way, and the business is yours.

The appointment of amateur organisers in such esoteric fields as international association meetings is easy to understand: the men are appointed for quite different qualities. What is more difficult to appreciate is the way in which major industrial companies appoint people without any previous experience to run important conferences. I remember one multi-national company, a pinnacle of business efficiency – and incidentally employing some very good friends of mine – which only ten years ago organised a major international engineers' conference, giving the sole responsibility to an executive who had never previously organised a darts match! That particular company does not make the same mistake now, but there are plenty that do.

Such organisers are in dire need of professional help, of the kind that any well-run hotel can give. For example, one organiser had a large group of German delegates and asked me whether we could prepare a German menu. 'Yes' I said, 'but I wouldn't recommend it. If I were in Munich, I wouldn't try their Yorkshire pudding, and the same is likely to apply in reverse.' Well, the client persevered and he produced a menu of German dishes he had obtained from another hotel. The budget for the menu was £3 a head and there was the suggested German menu facing me. 'I can't alter my opinion,' I told the organiser, 'but if you'd like that menu we can certainly serve it. But you can't have it for £3. It's only worth £2!' The other hotel did not get the business and we did not serve a German menu. What had been achieved was the creation of a credibility gap between the client and the competitive hotel, and the presentation of a golden nugget of proof that we were going to protect the client's interests at all costs.

Dinners

It is a stimulating – but rare – experience to deal with a client who really understands the business. I did once meet a client who was totally competent in organising dinners. He had the responsibility for a large communications company which, at the time, was trying to land some enormous contracts. Very important people were invited on inspection trips and this particular client was responsible for ensuring that they were well satisfied with their entertainment – of every description. He walked in to the hotel, looked at the banqueting room, sat me down and told me precisely what he wanted, including the service of cheese before the dessert – which is classically correct – but the only time that it has been specified in my experience. He then stood up without asking the price, and walked out again. There was nothing to say and nothing which needed elaborating, but a man of that ability is very rare.

The vast majority of clients by contrast worry a great deal about their lack of knowledge in the banqueting area. They worry that they will be cheated on drink consumption, that nothing will be ready on time, that this whole military-style operation will deteriorate into a rout and an ignominious retreat.

The position of the organiser is often unenviable. The mother of the bride will notice every minute shortcoming during the event and see it as a glaring error, horribly obvious to every sneering guest (on his side of the family of course!). A deluge of congratulations from all directions will not reassure her ('Well, they've got to say that, haven't they?') and she will go dramatically into a decline. It is hardly any better for the company organiser. Often landed with an unwanted responsibility by his director, scrutinised by a fair sprinkling of top brass on the night, not to mention the possibility of the wives commenting to his own fair lady, the poor fellow is bound to be on tenterhooks. Why, the efficiency of the hotel management could be all that stands between him and unemployment. Certainly in America, with their giant incentive trips, a disaster really will result on occasions in the dismissal of the man in charge. When such people are relying on hotel staff they do not personally control – and sometimes on hotels in a foreign country – it is not surprising that they worry.

We in the hotel business don't do enough to stop the client worrying. For instance, it is seldom standard procedure that, when a customer arrives, any member of staff in the banqueting room should immediately go to find the Banqueting or Duty Manager. This is vital, because many clients arrive early and see the room in the process of being set up for the evening. Having no idea how quickly this can be done, they survey the shambles as they might look at the foundations of a building not due to be occupied for months to come. They then assume that there is no chance of the room looking its best by the time the first guests arrive, panic, and need reassuring by a senior member of staff that all is well and in hand. This is part of selling, because it is part of the creation of confidence. A client who has confidence in his supplier takes that into account when he is approached to move his business elsewhere.

Probably the most common mistake in banquet selling takes place immediately after the event. At innumerable dinners, as the organiser is about to leave, the Banqueting Manager asks him if everything has been to his satisfaction and if he can pencil in the booking for the following year. The client invariably answers 'yes' to both questions, and the Banqueting Manager congratulates himself on another job well done. And that is the message he communicates to the General Manager if he is asked. What can be wrong with that?

Now let us suppose, for the sake of discussion, that the dinner was a total disaster. The organiser, horrified at the standards he sees around him, has had a dreadful evening. But at last the whole ghastly event is drawing to a close and he can leave the debacle. He heads for the door with his wife or a couple of colleagues, and along comes the culprit responsible for all his problems – the Banqueting Manager. And this man has the nerve to ask him, 'Was everything all right?' The organiser is furious, but he doesn't want to have any sort of argument in front of his wife and guests, nor to tackle the problem at the end of a long evening when he has had a few drinks and might say something he will regret later. He can always tell the Banqueting Manager exactly what he thinks of him when he is restored and refreshed, so he simply replies, 'Yes'. Would he like to make a provisional booking for next year? Since everybody knows that a provisional booking can be cancelled at any time without obligation, why not? The alternative is to decline and have the Banqueting Manager enquire there and then why not. That might develop into just the row the organiser wants to avoid in public.

So whether the evening was a great success or a total failure, the answer to the questions will most likely be the same. What is more, I have known many cases where a provisional booking of this dubious nature has been put in the Banqueting Book and definite bookings have been turned down because 'the booking we had last year is coming again'. It is only when the booking is checked because, inexplicably, the confirmation has failed to arrive, that the Banqueting Manager gets fobbed off with some excuse about a change of plans.

No salesman worth his salt is put off by a client who says that he has already made a *provisional* booking elsewhere. It is only when there is a definite booking that he knows he is going to have to wait till the following year for another attempt to obtain the business. Neither is the salesman put off when his own Banqueting Manager tells him that there is a provisional booking for the date he wants. He should always insist that the client with the provisional booking either makes up his mind to confirm the reservation definitely or releases the space for the customer who will do so.

How to Sell Banquets

There are, of course, any number of other aspects of a dinner which concern the organiser, the menu being the most obvious. Here we are dealing with the correct selling approach, which is always to keep in mind, first and foremost, that the client is usually out of his depth. You must take advantage of the opportunities, which come up again and again, to make him feel more at ease.

Luncheons

The factor which usually worries the client most about a luncheon is whether it is going to finish on time. The British do not favour the continental habit of taking hours and hours for lunch, nor, in fairness, the American habit of not eating such a meal at all if they can possibly avoid it. The British waver between the two attitudes and then worry! In the shortest period of time possible they try to pack in a cocktail party, a banquet and a meeting – for there are invariably speeches as well. As a result the organiser is always concerned that the luncheon will overrun its time; not that he personally, has anything else to do that afternoon. He plans to leave only after the last guest, tie up any loose ends with the Banqueting Manager and relax with a deep sigh of relief. His nightmare is that everybody else will leave before the end because the luncheon has overrun, and the guest speaker will then be on his feet, addressing an empty sea of dishevelled tables. Not a pretty sight!

To gain his confidence, the manager has to reassure the organiser that this is always his prime concern as well, to see that the timetable is adhered to rigidly. If the client accepts the reassurance, he need have no fears on that score; the manager has again imprinted professionalism and understanding of his problems on the customer's mind. He has also widened the credibility gap between the client and any other competitive hotel, which has not emphasised the point and may, therefore, be thought fallible in that direction.

The points made about dinners apply also to lunches, but the timing factor is not normally so important for a dinner.

Cocktail Parties

An invitation to the average cocktail party, is in my opinion, a fate worse than death! With nowhere to sit, your back inevitably starts to ache, and your ears prove increasingly ineffectual in deciphering, in the hubbub, the conversation of your neighbour. A combination of alcohol and animal heat makes you steadily more uncomfortable as the event progresses, your digestion is not helped by the absence of proper food, and little business can be done because serious talking is impossible. Thankfully for the hotel industry these self-evident facts have conspicuously failed to get through to the great British

20

public, and long may that continue!

Organisers of cocktail parties have two major problems; first, that the bill should be within their budget even in this uncontrolled bout of hospitality. Second, that the guests should remember the next day whose party they have attended. The control of the budget can be done by time – it is important not to let the party go on after the time it was scheduled to finish – and by measuring the drinks. Glasses, brimful of what is effectively money, are discarded with gay abandon as a guest spots somebody else he wanted to meet across the room. With drinks, as with buses, there's always another one coming! The effect on the bill and the sobriety of the staff afterwards we all know; measuring drinks is the solution.

A word of warning here, though: the first time I handled a cocktail party for a motor company, I kept clearly in mind that the bill must be reasonable so that the firm would come back again. So I told the staff to measure the drinks. The organiser took one look at the somewhat shallow level of the liquid in the glasses and rushed over to hiss at me, 'Doubles, you fool! Doubles!' Having spent umpteen million pounds on retooling the factory, and desperately anxious to sell large quantities of motor cars to his guests, the question of whether he spent another few hundred pounds on the drinks was totally insignificant. Cocktail parties, like any other banquet, demand that you find out the purpose before making your recommendations.

The task of getting the guest to remember whose party he has attended is a green light for the production of gimmicks. There are many industries where cocktail parties are two a penny – airlines, exhibition weeks, Spring and Autumn fashion shows – and for these events particularly the organiser desperately needs something unusual. In the chapter on creative banqueting, a number of possibilities in this area is examined: one example will suffice to make the point now. It concerns a lunch to decide the winner of the Buttonhole Flower of the Year competition. If this particular event does not rank in your mind with the Cup Final or the Boat Race, I should perhaps explain that a chain of multiple tailors was trying to get some free editorial publicity, and their P.R. company had dreamed up this competition; their thought process had linked a buttonhole with good tailoring. All the right guests of honour had been invited to act as judges – Nubar Gulbenkian and Stirling Moss, I remember, were amongst them – and the problem was to get the event the necessary publicity. We were able to provide the missing ingredient and get it in every newspaper the next day by simply recommending to the client a dish called a *Salade Mikado*. This is a reasonably complicated hors d'oeuvres decorated with edible chrysanthemum petals, and the reaction of Mr Gulbenkian, a noted gourmet in his time, to the delights of eating flowers was newsworthy. Only hoteliers know you can eat flowers, and a suggestion

21

of this kind will be received, by the right client, with open arms. Incidentally, there is an additional advantage in that the likelihood of any guest complaining that your *Salade Mikado* isn't up to scratch, is remote!

Product Launches

There are few more crucial types of function to the customer than the product launch. When so much money has been devoted to developing a new product, when the employment of so many people depends on its being successful, when indeed the viability of the company may depend on it, getting the launch off on the right foot is vital. We all know that a new product should be written about entirely on its merits; but it is a fact that, if the party to launch it is a terrible foul-up, the guests who suffered may equate the product with the entertainment. Unfair, perhaps, but it has happened.

The organiser is concerned firstly about the appearance of the product in your room, and secondly about the quality of your banqueting. This is one occasion when a strong theme in your banqueting room can be a disadvantage, because it can clash with the appearance of the product. A streamlined, gleaming white, twenty-first century refrigerator doesn't gain much from being displayed in a Victorian 'Gothic' ballroom. The organiser will want his product to dominate the room, and not vice versa. You must be on the lookout for this problem area and identify early on how the client regards the decor *vis-à-vis* what he wants to display in it.

Only when the client is satisfied that he can get the product into the room, that it will look good there, and that there is a satisfactory supply of whatever water, electricity, gas or anything else it consumes, can you move on to the quality of your cuisine and service. You should know about the technical requirements of a product launch in that machinery, for example, sometimes needs power supplies greater than the hotel normally provides. The Electricity Boards will run in a special power line for you – for which you charge the client – but the power line should not be regarded as some perverse customer peccadillo; without the right technical back-up, the product might not perform. Incidentally, it is also a point worth watching that the hire charge for the room should not necessarily include the electricity used by the product. If you are running a bank of new computers, for instance, the cost of the electricity used during the launch might easily be well in excess of the normal total rental charge.

When you get on to the catering aspects of a product launch, imaginative quality is likely to be more important than the cost. This is where you can use sugar work or ice work if it is appropriate. Make the model in chestnut purée or ice-cream, for instance, and it might well get more photographic editorial publicity for the client than even the genuine photograph.

A product launch should be treated like a military operation. Of all banqueting, this may justifiably be considered the most important to the client; it is not a subject for flippancy and you should discuss every minute aspect of it very carefully and seriously. No matter how informal and jolly the occasion might appear on the day, this can only be the result of thorough preparation. The organiser wants the hotel to be as wholly committed to the operation as he is.

Exhibitions

There are two types of exhibition; a stock room hired by an individual company, and the exhibition of a trade association. In both cases, part of the hotel is being converted into a shop-window for the client. A product launch is usually designed primarily for the press, but an exhibition is for buyers. Every exhibition organiser knows that he is going to have to disrupt the normal life of the hotel to a greater or lesser extent. He is usually prepared to pay for the privilege, but he doesn't want the hotel to imagine that running an exhibition is as simple as letting a bedroom for the night or arranging a dinner.

There are any number of difficulties an exhibition organiser brings with him; getting bulky material into the room; setting up at night; security; storing bedroom furniture if the exhibition is to make use of bedrooms; putting up large notice boards; dealing with large numbers of visitors who may come at any time of the day; and so on. The organiser knows that an exhibition is a complicated affair which can disturb the hotel's normal clientèle. He needs reassuring that you realise that, too, and are not going to put difficulties in his way. The sort of objections an exhibition organiser doesn't want to be faced with are, 'You can't deliver material after ten o'clock in the evening because the neighbours complain'; 'You can't stick anything on the walls or door frames'; 'It will be difficult to provide refreshments throughout the day'; and 'Exactly how many people do you expect?' The exhibition organiser is, first and foremost, interested in co-operation from the hotel in what is for him an imprecise business. He doesn't know how many visitors to expect, but he does want them well looked after if they come.

The man organising an exhibition has other problems too. He doesn't know how many stands he can sell, but he will want the largest possible option because he wants as many exhibitors as possible. As he is going to spend a lot of time and money trying to sell your facilities for you, it seems only reasonable for you to be as flexible as possible in return. Price is not normally a problem. The organiser is going to mark up your charges by a high percentage to cover the overheads of advertising and publicity, stand building and brochures; your charges will not be a large proportion of the selling price.

How to Sell Banquets

Above all, the organiser expects to deal with professionals in the hotel. He has a great deal to do in setting up the exhibition, and the exhibitors have a limited time to display their goods. They want to spend their time profitably on the stand, not wasting endless hours getting in and out of the hotel.

As you can see the factors that really matter to a banquet customer can differ very widely. Uniformity of approach is therefore impossible, but most hotels do indeed deal with banquets according to a set routine. Time and again the letter responding to an enquiry carries almost exactly the same wording, whether the subject is a sales conference or a wedding; the rooms are available, the prices are such-and-such, the specimen menus are enclosed, and we hope to hear from the customer again. On receiving such a vague letter, most customers have to start the laborious task of fitting your information into their picture of what matters. It is only natural that when they receive a letter from one hotel which immediately homes in on the points they feel to be important, that is the hotel most likely to secure the business.

The Initial Stages

Some readers may remember Lobby Ludd. Using this alias he represented a national newspaper in the 1930s and visited various seaside towns during the summer. If you saw Lobby Ludd and had the newspaper with you, you could win a prize. Thousands of people were on the look-out for Lobby Ludd, as one might look for a rainbow or a patch of blue sky in the midst of a storm.

The banqueting enquiry can be likened to another version of Lobby Ludd. It represents the lucky win, the profit that walks in off the street, the pot of gold found at the end of the rainbow. Often it is pure chance that the client is prepared to consider your hotel, and he gives you one fleeting opportunity to secure his business. Like a rare butterfly, he alights momentarily on the bush near your net, and without careful stalking he will disappear for ever. Does he get that careful stalking? This is what should happen following an enquiry. Compare your own method.

There are three ways for a client to contact you, by letter, by telephone and in person:

The Written Enquiry

The correct way of responding to a letter of enquiry is to telephone the client, not to reply by letter. There are two reasons for this.

1. If the client has written to other hotels at the same time, your telephone call reaches the client first. He effectively listens to you before anybody else. You jump the queue.

2. The client's letter is seldom sufficiently detailed for you to decide on your selling strategy.

A typical letter is illustrated here (Fig. 1). As you can see, there is great difficulty in identifying the type of dinner which Mr Gibbons wants to give. Is he anxious to keep to a strict budget? Or are his objectives so important that he is much more concerned with the result than the cost? Whether you emphasise your quality or your value for money depends on the answer to that question. If you emphasise quality to a man on a strict budget, he will equate quality with a high price. If you talk about value for money to a man who has bigger fish to fry than keeping to a budget, you will make your facilities sound cheap and nasty.

You also need to discover whether the dinner is to be formal or informal – another point the letter doesn't illuminate. For a formal dinner you would talk about your high standard of service, your ability to prepare the classic dishes and the elegance of your banqueting rooms – not in so many elaborate words but getting over the right impression. If it is an informal occasion, you would talk about your skill at putting on a party, your cosy, jolly room and the fun it can all be. You must establish the mood and purpose of the function before you can select your approach.

In the initial stages of selling banquets, any letter you write can be helpful only in setting down details which have already been agreed with the client. For you it is, at best, a form of confirmation, but not of communication. The letter gives you no chance to see the client's reaction to your suggestions – a serious drawback compared with a personal interview. It forces you to state facts before you know whether those facts are the ones the client wants to hear. For example, in a letter you might state a minimum charge for a menu. Now minimum charges are almost a standard feature of our banqueting policy, and yet their existence does not stand up to logical examination. If, for sake of example, a particularly hard-drinking group want a menu which is £1 below the minimum charge, it would still be highly profitable to sell the meal at that price because the profit on the sale of drinks would easily compensate for the loss of food revenue. Indeed, a minimum-priced menu does not show the hotel a profit at all if there is no sale of drinks, because then the menu alone has to carry the overheads of rent, rates, gas, electricity and so on. At the end of the day only the contribution of the profit on drinks balances the hotel budget.

Our insistence therefore on minimum prices for a menu – 'Our menu prices start at £3.50' – is an error. What we should be asking ourselves is what is the minimum profit we want to make out of the room on the night in question. That profit will differ between a Friday night in December and a Monday night in early January, between a popular and unpopular banqueting night. Therefore, before you quote the minimum price you want for the menu, you need to know the total budget the client has set aside for the function. The minimum price for school mistresses would have to be higher than the minimum for travel agents or licensed victuallers who do like a noggin or six!

There will be occasions when a letter has to be written as a selling document.

Figure 1. A typical initial enquiry ▶

Profit & Incum Ltd
17 Rainbow Street, Giftchester. Telephone 073-9898

HG/MR   January 10th

The Manager,
King William Hotel,
Barchester.

Dear Sir,

   I would like to hold a dinner for about
50 guests on Wednesday, March 9th, and I
should be grateful if you would let me
know whether you have a suitable room
available.

   Could you also please let me have some
sample menus and a copy of your wine list.

                    Yours faithfully,

                    Harold Gibbons,
                    Director

How to Sell Banquets

Perhaps the client wants a proposal to be put before a committee meeting, he might not have time to visit the hotel for some weeks and wants to get on with his planning. In such cases you can still make a telephone call first, but the letter will have to follow before the client makes up his mind. We will come back to the construction of letters later; but wherever possible in the initial stages avoid this particular method of communication.

Telephoning the Client

Before you pick up the telephone to speak to the client, you should write down the questions to which you want answers. The purpose of the telephone call is threefold:

1. To reach the client before your competitors,
2. To ask the client to visit the hotel – preferably for lunch or dinner with you if the party is of a substantial size,
3. To gather the maximum amount of information about the party before you commit yourself to an approach on why you should be given the business.

Some of the greatest American salesmen way back in the 1950s taught me to use the telephone rather than write letters – the American Hilton men were particularly good at this. One of my happiest memories was some fifteen years later when a multi-national company were holding a major international conference in London. The letter of enquiry came in, I telephoned as usual, invited the client to lunch and agreed a price for a large slice of the business. I couldn't do it all and some weeks later I happened to bump into the Sales Manager for the London Hilton. I knew that he, too, must have received the enquiry and I asked him whether he had got any business out of it. 'I'm still waiting for a reply to my letter,' he said, to my great satisfaction.

The reason for inviting the client to lunch or dinner is primarily to get one and half hours of his undivided attention. To that extent the invitation is a modest bribe. No interruptions from telephones, no worries that the work is piling up while he talks to you: you get his full attention. It is also a perfectly legitimate technique when buying a product in bulk to sample it first; a wine tasting, a free sample of new toothpaste in the supermarket, or a small sachet of a new car polish are only a few examples of this in other industries. Any client with a large banquet to place is stupid to take your cooking on trust, even if the standard of the restaurant can sometimes have very little bearing on your ability to run a banquet. The client has to judge by some yardstick, and the restaurant is the best available. If on the telephone the client sounds as if he is in a cheerful mood, I might well couch the invitation to lunch or dinner in terms of, 'If you're thinking of inflicting our cooking on so many of your colleagues, you ought to risk being poisoned yourself first'. This is one example of under-selling, an important technique because many business clients are well accustomed to – and suspicious of – the all-embracing claims of salesmen to perfection in their product. For somebody to denigrate their product in a jocular manner can be a pleasant change.

Although it is less of a bribe in our industry than in any other to offer free hospitality, the client might still consider that an unseemly bribe is being offered. As an insurance, you can couch your invitation in such a way that you automatically provide him with an excuse for accepting. It will be on the lines of that great Cadbury's campaign, 'Have some chocolate; you deserve it'. The guilt complex of customers when eating fattening chocolate is assuaged by showing them initially working hard, then getting their reward of a bite of Fruit and Nut. In that view, another way of offering the invitation is, 'I don't want to take up too much of your working day. Why not come to lunch; you've got to eat'. The client can accept the implication that he will be flogging himself to death at his desk all day, and will even continue to work at lunch-time, discussing his function with you.

Now what information do you want from the client when you first tele-phone him? You need to know:

1. The purpose of the function,
2. The total budget the client has set aside for it,
3. The degree of sophistication of the guests,
4. The technical knowledge of the client,
5. Any details of timing, numbers or other elementary facts which might have been missing from the initial letter, as they affect your ability to accept the function in the first place.

Why do you need to know these things? The purpose of the function gives you an indication of the quality the client wants, and the importance of the event to the company. All functions are important, but the man organising the Chairman's annual dinner is likely to be rather more anxious than the one arranging the retirement party for Mr Bristowe in Accounts; unjustifiable but realistic. The degree of anxiety of the client is important because you can sell banquets on occasions simply on the basis that the client is safe with you; you will stand like Horatio on the bridge protecting the client with the sword of your expertise from the dire fate which will befall him if he mucks up the Chairman's party. The same can apply to a mother arranging the wedding of her only daughter, as we have seen.

You want to know the budget in order to decide the potential profitability of the function. Some hotels set minimum numbers on a popular banqueting night but, like the minimum cost of the menu, this is a false yardstick. The total bill is the criterion, because it is the most accurate way to assess your profit.

How to Sell Banquets

The degree of sophistication of the guests matters because it predetermines your approach to the client. For example, only a few years ago you would never have suggested avocados for a staff party: far too sophisticated a taste. You would not suggest trout either, because the dissection of a trout takes skill, and too many unsophisticated clients would be likely to finish up with a mouthful of small bones, having attacked the fish from the outside instead of opening it up down the middle. Offering the Chairman steak and kidney pie would also have been a mistake – even if he loved it – because it would have been thought to lack dignity, if not succulence.

The technical knowledge of the client determines another aspect of your approach. Is your role to have overtones of guardian angel, are you going to play Sancho Panza to his Don Quixote, the faithful servant to the impresario, or Master of Ceremonies? One trouble with far too many banqueting salesmen is that they can play only a limited number of roles. They can usually manage the deferential and the guardian angel. But other roles should include the party giver, the public relations expert, the set designer, the adopted uncle of the bride who happens to be in the hotel business, the unexpected member of the club and the wizard of minor orgies. Which part the client is hiring you to play, in order to reassure himself that his banquet is going to be a success, depends to a large extent on his own knowledge of your business.

The elementary facts need establishing at the outset. If the numbers are too large, for instance, you might not be able to handle the party at all. You also seek to establish less fundamental problems which still have to be overcome. For example, if there is to be dancing, you might receive the comment, 'Yes, and we do like a large dance floor because it's a young crowd and they like to get on to the floor'. If you have a dance floor which is small for the numbers involved, you are prewarned that you are going to have to deal with this shortcoming in your facilities – perhaps by swapping another booking to another room.

Let us establish at this point that you do not have the ideal product for every type of party – nor do you need it, because nobody else has it either. There are always shortcomings, and everybody buys the lesser of a number of evils. When management get too involved in their own hotel, and love it like a child of their own creation, this fundamental fact tends to get forgotten to the detriment of their selling. They try to prove to the client that everything is perfect, which even the average client knows to be highly unlikely. They try to prove the unprovable – that their intimate dance floor could comfortably accommodate the massed bands of the Brigade of Guards. The client might like a dance floor like a parade ground, but there is often room for compromise in this as in many other things. What there is no room for, is a doubt in the client's mind that the salesman is telling him the truth. As Caesar wisely said, 'Yon

Cassius doth protest too much'. Unlike Caesar, clients take precautions with managers who oversell. It is worth remembering that the hotel doesn't have to be perfect, and claims of perfection can be self-defeating.

So you pick up the telephone and call the client. Never get your secretary to call the client for you. She can call the company, but then you must take over when the telephonist answers. Otherwise the client may pick up the phone and hear your secretary coo, 'One moment please. I have Mr Snodgrass for you'. The client stops the meeting, loses his train of thought whilst dictating, breaks off his conversation to wait for you to come on the telephone, and all in order to hear you say that you want to sell him something; ugh! There is no finer way of ruining a sale right at the very beginning.

In fact, it is not always easy to get to speak to the client. Obviously he might be out, away from the office for days, or tied up. As he has written to you, the likelihood is that he will take the call if he is available. If his secretary is the sort who vets his calls and only puts through the people she thinks he would want to talk to, then you must persuade her that you are in that category. 'He wrote to me' is a good start, but that reason can leave you open to her reply, 'He only wanted you to send him some sample menus. Would you please write and do that'. Therefore the correct approach is, 'He wrote to me, but there are a few points I need to clarify'. Unless the secretary is particularly able, she will not feel competent to decide whether the letter was sufficiently detailed or not, and you will get through. If she asks what the questions are, be amicable but make the questions lengthy and very technical. For example, 'We're likely to have the Beaujolais Nouveau in at that time, but I think Mr Gibbons may well prefer the Chateauneuf du Pape.' If that isn't enough, try 'Do you know if he wants the Ramon Allones Ideales or the Upmann glass jars?'

Notice the phrase, 'I need to clarify,' not, 'There were a few points which weren't made clear'. 'Clarify' is a word which offers no criticism of the writer, only a request for more information. To say that something isn't clear is to criticise the writer and imply that he should have made it clear. You might think that this is a tiny point; so it is, and there are thousands of tiny points which – correctly handled – will improve your batting average at banquet selling.

One word in the wrong place can raise doubts in the client's mind and undo the hard work of hours. That is why a good salesman does not like anyone else in the hotel to be present when he is selling; a colleague can say something disastrous simply because he doesn't know what is in the salesman's mind. For example, the use of the phrase, 'Oh, I don't think we can do that'. The correct phrase is, 'Now, how are we going to do that?' Kicking a colleague under the table is not the answer, because you might kick the client by mistake! As you will see, a salesman's approach to a client's suggestions may be extremely convoluted and difficult to follow for another member of the hotel's management. A good rule, unless a rapport of considerable strength has been set up over a long period by two salesmen, is for only one person to do the talking.

If the client is unavailable, find out when he *will* be in. If it is not before the next day, remember that other hotels may be writing and the letters will be on the client's desk when he arrives next morning. That doesn't mean that you now have to write. The disadvantages of writing remain just as valid. It does mean that to jump the queue you have to telephone him early in the morning so that you speak to him before he opens his post. Timing is obviously vital here, as indeed it is in many other aspects of banquet selling.

So now you have announced your name and the name of your hotel to the secretary and she says that she is putting you through. Talking to a stranger on the telephone is very much like communicating on television when you are reading the news; there are certain words you definitely want the client to hear, and there are others which are less important. The important ones get emphasised; thus, 'Good morning, Mr **Gibbons** (people like the sound of their own name). My name is **Derek** Taylor (starting a process which should lead eventually to first-name terms), The King William **Hotel**. You remember you **wrote** to us about the **dinner** you want to hold on **March 9th**.' And you then stop to give the client a chance to enter into the conversation.

Now notice a number of points even after these brief opening remarks. The client should have heard his own name, your first name, the name of the hotel, the fact that your call refers to a letter he wrote about a dinner, and the date. These key words will attract his attention away from what he is doing. He will recognise that the call is one he initiated by writing, and therefore he will be amenable to dealing with the matter. But he may want to delay the conversation because he is busy. Your stopping early gives him the chance to do so before he becomes irritated with your conversation. You can tell from his first words – relaxed, on-the-ball, irritable, surprised, impatient, pleased, etc. – whether you have chosen a good moment. If you have not, you must identify when would be better, because you want the client to listen to you in a favourable frame of mind. Selling to people when they want to be doing something else is bad technique. We are not in industries like life insurance, where I suspect nobody ever wants to talk to a salesman; in hotel selling the reception can be very good so long as one is sensitive to the possibility that the client has other things on his mind.

The delivery of your opening remarks is also important. It is no use bumbling, 'um-ing and 'er-ing. You must be fluent, and the delivery should be at a moderate speed until you hear the reaction. From the speed of the client's conversation, you get the key for your own. If a client talks slowly, don't rush words at him. If he races through conversations, try to keep up with him. Your voice must sound confident and pleasantly businesslike. Don't snap at him, but don't put oodles of syrup into your voice either. Your normal voice delivery when talking to the local greengrocer should do fine.

When starting a conversation, you should assume that it will take no more than a few minutes. This provides you with the necessary sense of urgency to get all your questions answered. Unless the client is particularly interested, he will be prepared to spare you only a few minutes at this point, and consequently you must get down to business straight away. Remarks like, 'It's a very nice day, isn't it?' are not going to help at all.

Assuming that the client says, 'Yes, I remember,' and sounds reasonably receptive, you can go on. 'Mr **Gibbons** (using the name again – he still likes the sound of it), I will, of **course,** let you have some sample **menus** and a **wine** list, but I **wonder** whether I could get a **little** more information about the dinner so that I can provide you with the right **suggestions**.' Why the particular choice of words? 'Of course' to reassure him that there is no problem in getting what he wants. 'Menus' and 'wine' to reassure him that you will send him the right things. 'Wonder' because you don't want him to feel that you take it for granted that he will spare the time to talk to you. 'Little' because he needs reassuring that talking to you won't take up too much time. 'Suggestions' because you are not trying to dictate to him, but simply to help.

Complicated, isn't it? But one must appreciate that words have very definite meanings, and you simply must use the right ones to get over your message. You may choose 'recommendations' rather than 'suggestions', 'a small amount' rather than 'little', but you should still be trying to get over the same ideas.

You stop again to give the client a chance to comment. A one-sided sales conversation where you do all the talking, is one which is going wrong. Why? Because there is no way that you are going to select exactly the right information to give the client simply on the basis of the scanty information he normally gives you. He has told you there will be fifty people, but are they employees or guests, V.I.P.s or lesser executives, dancers or watchers, drinkers or abstemious, trenchermen or weightwatchers? If the client just answers 'Yes' or 'No', you will be on the telephone for ever trying to extract the really important facts. So you want the client to contribute to the discussion, to use the framework of information that you are giving him to visualise his picture of what his ideal function is going to be like.

If he is too polite to interrupt your presentation, be sure to stop to give him the chance to do so at regular intervals. If he makes no comment, ask him questions. If his answers are monosyllabic, draw him out with questions like, 'What have been your major concerns about the success of the dinner in the past?' or, 'What particular mood would you like to achieve?' In other words, ask the kind of questions that make it difficult for him to give short answers, and then listen intently so that he knows that you *are* interested. On the telephone, use short phrases like, 'I see', or 'I understand', and remember to put a smile into your voice. He can't see the smile of relief on your face that you are talking to the right man, and that he is willing to listen to you. The pleasure has to come out in the voice. As you are quite likely to be nervous, because there is a lot of natural tension in selling, try to relax physically before you pick up the telephone. Sit in an easy chair or even put your feet on the office desk, as I used to. The prize is for getting the business, not for looking efficient if somebody comes into the room.

If the client asks 'What can I tell you?'; put your questions in a logical pattern. You establish what the reason for the function is, and the other details you need. You also make a mental decision whether you want the business or not. There are occasions when the answer is that you do not because, for example, the budget may be small and the numbers inadequate for your large room on a popular night. If you do decide you want the business, then you need more of the client's time to make a proper presentation. At that point, try to persuade him to come to the hotel to see the room, invite him for lunch or dinner if he can spare the time, otherwise for a morning or afternoon visit. If he will not come to you because he is too busy, you have to offer to go to see him.

He may suggest that as he is, personally, too tied up, he will send a more junior executive to see the room. Beware of this trap. Your presentation to the new man will be to the non-decision maker. Therefore your message will be relayed to the client in a less able way than you could have done it, face to face, yourself. In such cases, say 'I'd be very glad to show Mr Smith around the hotel, but as the final responsibility is yours, could I also call on you to explain the more technical details personally'. The implied flattery that only he would appreciate the finer points, should do the trick. If he replies that he has every confidence in the judgement of his colleague, he is sending a specialist and not a junior.

In order to assess whether it would be worth his while to come to visit you or to make an appointment for you to call at his office, the client is likely to try to get some hard information on whether your hotel would be suitable. If he can decide that you are not the answer to his problem, he is going to save an unnecessary journey. For your part, you are not keen for him to make up his mind on that point until you have made a presentation in person, so you must try to stall. The invitation to lunch may be sufficient, because to decide against you is to lose an excellent lunch. If the client is more professional than that, you must give the impression that whatever problems he raises are either easily solvable or will be overcome.

The Telephone Enquiry

A large proportion of banqueting enquiries are made by a client telephoning you, rather than vice versa. A considerable number of banquets also finish at that point, because of bad handling. The ideal is simplicity itself; the client wants to talk to you in order to spend money, and you want to talk to him. Therefore he rings you up and you speak to him. Only it doesn't always work that way. He rings you up and the telephonist has to have time to deal with his call. She has to find you and you have to have the time to talk to the client. In carrying out the exercise, the client can be left holding on for some time if the telephonist is busy, if you can't be found, or if nobody answers your extension. He can be interrogated about his business by the telephonist, your assistant and/or your secretary until – you would be surprised how often it happens to the client – he gets fed up and tries somewhere else. Quite obviously people do not set out to irritate a man who wants to buy a function from them. If it happens, therefore, it happens by accident.

How can these disasters be avoided? There are a number of rules which help. Firstly, tell the telephonist to put everybody through to you who asks, and to do so without enquiring their name, the name of their company or anything else. That will eliminate a lot of the delay. Why doesn't that happen already? Because the manager will then get people put through to him whom he doesn't want to speak to. This may be inconvenient but it is far better to deal with a few unnecessary calls than not to get the important ones quickly. When managers say to me, 'But the caller might be a salesman!', I always reply that I would rather treat the salesmen like customers than the customers like salesmen. Another excuse is, 'I like to get out the file before I speak to the caller, so that I am up to date'. That is usually irrelevant. You can hardly know from a file what the client wants to talk to you about. The main reason for these excuses is so that the manager can avoid awkward calls; in having such a policy he is putting his own comfort ahead of the benefit to the hotel.

Next, always tell your secretary where you are when you leave the office. This involves you in a fair amount of personal discipline, but if you don't do it she will not be able to find you, and then the delay occurs. You can tell your secretary to take the caller's name and telephone number and say that you will ring him back, but this, too, is dangerous. Suppose that the client has rung the next hotel on his list and got what he wanted *before* you ring back? It is no use saying he should have been more patient. He is spending the money and can do what he likes. The worst thing, of course, is when the client is told, 'He isn't in at the moment. *Can you ring back?*' Why ever should he ring back when he wants to spend money with you, and you are so badly organised that he can't reach you and is told to try again?

How to Sell Banquets

Train other management to deal effectively with banquet enquiries. It is possible to train all kinds of people to be good banquet salesmen. Even quite junior staff can be taught at least the initial fundamentals of taking a call. Tell them to reassure the client that your hotel can cater for the numbers, that the date is available, and that you can be relied upon to ring as soon as you return. Make sure that they get the name and telephone number correctly – absolutely without fail – and have a pleasant manner on the telephone. Those are the only things needed to keep a client happy while they wait to talk to you. You must remember, however, that one person can only do so much: the more management you train to sell, the more ground you can cover.

Banqueting Books (Diaries)

The phrase 'the date is available' is very simple. Studying many banqueting books to discover whether the date is, in fact, available is often very difficult. For an industry which takes great care to set down liquor and food stocks, casual wages and print item inventories accurately and in great detail, we seem positively cavalier in the way we keep the banqueting book.

I remember an occasion early in my career when it had taken me almost three years to get a client to the point where he offered me a piece of business; when I rang the hotel, I was told that the only room of the right size wasn't available. Out of sheer disappointment I asked the banqueting manager why not, and made him go through his bookings for the day in question. It transpired that the booking for the room I wanted was provisional – not definite at all – and that I could have it after all. If I had not been persistent, the three years' work would have gone for nothing. I learned at that point never to assume that a banqueting book was correctly detailed.

On many occasions, business is really lost by simply refusing a date which is really available. Other common errors in banqueting books are the provisional bookings of annual functions from year to year, without knowing whether the client intends to return. Other enquiries are turned down, until the client eventually cancels and leaves you with a vacancy, too late to be filled. Another common error is to forget to put in the time the function starts or finishes. If this happens, another function might be refused on the wrong assumption that the room is in use. Without knowing the time a conference finishes, for instance, you cannot know what time you can accept a booking for a dinner in the same room.

Every function entry in the banqueting book should have the following information:
1. The name of the organiser.
2. The organisation (if there is one).

3. The telephone number.
4. The type of business.
5. The numbers to be catered for.
6. Whether the booking is provisional or definite.
7. The room allocated.
8. The date of the enquiry.
9. The starting and finishing times.
10. Accommodation needed.

With this information you can use the book effectively. If you need a date where a provisional booking already exists, you have the details in the book to ring the organiser without referring to any other source of information. The alternative is to find the file, which might be in another room, and this wastes time. By knowing the date of the enquiry, you know when you should contact the client the following year for the same order. People's business decisions tend to run to pattern, and if they settle down to arrange the dinner in September this year, they will more likely than not do the same next year. The date of the initial enquiry also enables you to see how long the provisional booking has been made. Even so, you should not necessarily suspect a provisional booking of being useless on the basis that it has been there a long time. You should chase the business at the correct time so that provisional bookings are converted into definite ones as quickly as possible.

It takes a certain amount of discipline to keep up a banqueting book properly, but the effort is repaid many times over by the additional revenue that accrues from simply not turning down business unnecessarily and from chasing it more effectively. The correct criterion by which to judge a properly kept-up banqueting book is whether the most junior member of the department can give a customer correct information on any date and any room.

Personal Enquiries

What happens when a client calls at your hotel in order to consider buying a function? It really is no different from walking into a car showroom to buy a motor car. The sums involved are often similar, so perhaps we might deal with the enquiry in a similar manner. We would expect the car salesman to be immediately available, to have all the time we need, and to be anxious to sell the vehicle. Is that what happens when a client calls at a hotel without an appointment? Not usually.

What usually happens is that he goes up to the hall porter or the reception desk and says that he would like to see the manager. At that point he is politely but firmly interrogated. What is his name, what is his organisation if any, and does he have an appointment? The porter then offers to give the manager the information to find out whether on that basis he will see the client. Whilst the interrogation and call to the manager is made, the client stands in the lobby as if he were at the Pearly Gates. All around him are guests who have been admitted and are obviously members of the club, and there he is, the client with an overcoat on, still at the desk and standing out like a sore thumb.

The impression which is so often given is that 'The manager doesn't see just anyone, you know' and, 'You may say you have an appointment but you look a bit suspicious to me, so I'll just check to see that you are not lying'. Those are hardly the right impressions to give a client at the beginning of his buying process, and the situation does not usually improve. The likelihood is that you will not be immediately available – for a casual caller this is not unreasonable – and so there is a delay. Often the client is simply told, 'The manager won't keep you long', and is left in the lobby, still out of place in his overcoat, to kick his heels for an indefinite period. The time specified by the phrase 'won't keep you long' is approximately the same length as a piece of string! No refreshment is offered the client though a seat usually is. Have you ever tried sitting in your overcoat in a strange hotel lobby? It is easy to imagine the atmosphere enjoyed by a cuckoo in someone else's nest.

The correct procedure therefore has to be established for the reception of expected or unexpected clients. The right way is as follows:

1. A member of staff should immediately offer to take the client's coat and invite him to take a seat.
2. He should take his name and say that he will tell the manager the client has arrived.
3. Give the client an accurate estimate of how long he might have to wait if you are not immediately available.
4. Offer the client a cup of tea or coffee in the lounge.

'But the caller might be a salesman,' comes the objection to this procedure. It is better to treat a salesman like a client, than a client like an unwelcome caller.

Consider the comparison between the interrogation procedure and the right one. If you had to choose between two car showrooms, which one would be most likely to obtain your business? In fact if the correct immediate welcome is given, a hotel might still get the business; even if its facilities were not quite as good as those of the opposition. The hotel is in competition with others, and any help or goodwill that can be gathered from the staff being that little more friendly or courteous may come in very useful in a close finish.

If you have had to keep the client waiting, always hurry towards him saying right at the beginning how sorry you are to have done so. If, by contrast, you just stroll up and ask how you can help, you give the impression that you do not care that he has been kicking his heels. The fact that he had no right to expect you to be immediately available is not the point. The object is to create the maximum goodwill as quickly as possible, and the impression that you have rushed to avoid keeping him waiting a moment longer than necessary is a good start. You might consider him unreasonable, but keep your mental eye firmly fixed on the fact that he can be as unreasonable as he likes, so long as he finishes up giving you the business.

Shake hands with him warmly and firmly. There is absolutely nothing worse at the outset of a meeting than a wet, cold handshake – a limp paw lifelessly held out. It is up to you to ensure that you grip his hand before his fingers close on yours.

As soon as you have established that he wants to talk business, take the client to a room where you can sit down, and offer him some refreshment. Do not offer alcohol except during licensing hours. This is not because of some obscure licensing law, but to avoid giving the impression that he must want a drink at any old time of day, or worse still that you need one. Don't offer plain biscuits either. In the morning offer a plate of chocolate biscuits, as well as such delicacies as bourbons, ginger snaps or a Danish pastry; in the afternoon, offer small sandwiches and a piece of cake. Don't just go through the motions of hospitality; try to be a little original so that he will compare the treatment he has received from you with the miserly behaviour of your competitor. It is the little touches that make the difference.

If you are taking the client to your office, try to ensure that you do not sit on one side of the desk and place him on the other. Such an arrangement makes the client feel like a supplicant in the headmaster's study. It is better to have two easy chairs and a coffee table if your office is large enough. If it is not, talk to clients in the lounge. You want them to relax and feel at home.

When you meet the client it is still your purpose to obtain the maximum information before committing yourself to a particular presentation. The difference between this occasion and the telephone call, however, is that you cannot so obviously take control of the conversation. You had the perfect excuse for doing so on the telephone; you had rung him for more information, so naturally you asked the questions. Now you have the client with you and *he* wants to ask the questions because he has to fit your hotel facilities into his buying requirements.

There are a lot of questions you don't mind being asked, questions about your strengths, whatever they are. What you don't want to discuss early in the conversation are your weaknesses: too small a dance floor, too high a price, a lack of soundproofing, or whatever. If the conversation looks like moving in those directions, you have to gently redirect it to another subject until the client is sufficiently pleased with what he has heard to put your shortcomings into perspective. If the first things that a client finds out are that the floor is too small, the room too noisy and the price too high, he doesn't go on. If he finds these things out after an hour of identifying why the room is ideal in other ways for his function, the problems are an irritant to him rather than a disaster. He will look for ways to overcome them, make allowances, and try to buy the product in spite of the drawbacks. If he gets the wrong impression at the beginning, he will try to criticise your good points in order to strengthen his decision not to buy because of your bad points.

So you must lead the conversation. What sort of framework will it have? In most hotels there is a sheet of paper called a Banqueting Enquiry Form – or something similar – which has room for all the details. A great many banquet salesmen start at the top and work down: name, address, telephone number, number of guests, and so on. This is useless as a selling guide. It works perfectly well if the guest definitely wants to buy; but if he is making up his mind, the questions need to be asked in the order the client finds important. If he is primarily concerned about the sound equipment, then that is the first question that should be covered. The problem arises when his major interest coincides with your major weakness. A secret war then breaks out with you endeavouring to stay off the subject without the client realising it. If he asks a straight question about the point that is actually your weakness, then of course you have to answer frankly. Otherwise he is irritated at not getting the answer and immediately suspects that you can't cope. But you can avoid this happening by interesting the client in any number of other facets of the function. You will appreciate that this demands the utmost concentration on your part, constantly checking whether the conversation is heading towards those submerged rocks of your banqueting defects on which your presentation may be going to founder.

So you collect information the way you do a jig-saw puzzle – you fit in the pieces as they come to hand and not in a set order. With a really professional salesman the client should never be aware of the selling process; it is like well applied make-up – there to enhance rather than to smother. I suppose the greatest compliment I was ever paid as a salesman was by a young lady who had given me an enormous amount of business in her capacity as manager of her company's hotel booking service. One day, after I had found her a room for a particularly difficult peak period, she asked me, 'What do you actually do for your company?' As far as she was concerned, I existed solely to help her do her job! And that is what a salesman should be – a help, an expert and hardly recognisable as a salesman.

There is all the difference in the world between taking control of the conversation and dominating it. If the client wants to do a lot of the talking, encourage him to do so, because there is useful information to be gleaned almost all the time. It is what he talks about rather than how much he talks that matters.

These, then, are the initial stages of a banquet sale. If you start off on the right foot, you have a much better chance of finishing the race at the head of the field.

Sales Presentation

3

The battle is now joined. There you are, just you and the client. If you are to win the battle, the client has to agree to buy. The odds seem uneven; there is no force you can bring to bear on the client. You cannot lock him up until he agrees to pay the ransom like Richard the Lionheart. You cannot blackmail him, threaten him or compromise him. All he has to do is to say 'No' and walk out. It looks like David and Goliath, but at least David had a sling. What has the salesman got?

It *is* an uneven contest, but against a professional salesman it is the client who is often at a hopeless disadvantage. The amateur buyer will usually be persuaded by the professional salesman to decide in his favour. In the wrong hands, it is rather like the performance of most politicians on television. You might not believe a word they say, but they can be so convincing, you still want to buy it.

The salesman does indeed have very powerful weapons. He understands what the client is trying to achieve and can show the client that those objectives will receive a powerful boost at his hotel. He understands his business so well that the client is confident that the hotel's participation in the event can be left with total safety in the salesman's hands. The client might still have to deal with the problems of the content of the sales conference, the details of the after-dinner speeches, the composition of the visual displays, but he can forget about the hotel's side of it. Once the details are agreed with the professional sales-man, the client feels that, in that area at least, he has no worries. Moreover people want to work with suppliers they like and the professional salesman is very likeable.

Think of a shop you often visit and of the person behind the counter. He understands your problems, is an expert on the goods he sells, and he is a nice fellow. It is a tremendous combination, but how does the salesman achieve it?

The essential secret is that he achieves it in a multitude of ways. The method he selects differs according to the type of client he is facing. The professional salesman can play as many roles as an impersonator. He is the kindly uncle to the young and inexperienced; the devoted follower of the strong leader; bags of fun to the party giver, and Black Rod to the organiser of dignified functions. For the professional, these roles are not play-acting, shallow and false; he draws for his behaviour pattern on different situations in his private life. He analyses how he behaves at a football match, with his grandfather, at a funeral, on a spree, with a loved one, or with his boss and he fits in with different clients by producing the right behaviour pattern. If this is play-acting, then most successful businessmen play-act – at board meetings, long service dinners, with their bosses, subordinates and at the office party. But it is not play-acting; it is the selection of the appropriate behaviour for each occasion. The professional salesman has the sensitivity to select the correct approach for each individual client.

Memories come flooding back to me of the Brigadier who, on the telephone, referred to his sales force as 'the chaps'. So when I met him, I wore a dark suit and well-polished shoes, I didn't slouch, and cocktails were agreed at 19.00 hours. The manager who accompanied me even wanted to refer to the hotel's candelabra as the Mess Silver, but we finally agreed this was going a bit too far! I remember a particular green suit I selected for clients who brought in Pop groups; the sort of client who, on being asked the quality of a hotel in those days, would reassure his own customer by telling them that, 'Man, it swings!' That is why I have always been very much against the old custom of management being dressed in a black jacket and striped trousers; it establishes an image which, if not appropriate for the type of client you are meeting, will take a lot of living down. The salesman wants to give a good impression – the right one – from the moment the client meets him. His appearance is part of that first impression.

Keep in mind as we go through a sales presentation the three objectives:
1. To contribute to the success of the client's function;
2. To establish expert knowledge;
3. To be likeable.

As I make the points, I will indicate the appropriate number beside them.

Let me introduce you to Mr R. H. Coxwell, Company Secretary of Canwe, Seldom & Co Ltd, manufacturers of electrical spare parts. Mr Coxwell is organising a dinner in March for 150 guests and has agreed to come to see our hotel. We have arrived at the hotel entrance at 12.55, and promptly at 1 o'clock a gentleman goes up to the porter and asks for Mr Taylor. You and I step forward, and the minimum time has elapsed before Mr Coxwell is reassured that he is at the right place and the man he has come to see is there (3). Who wants to worry on either of those two scores?

'Good morning, Mr Coxwell. I'm Derek Taylor, and this is my colleague, Dere Reader.' Not 'my assistant', which might well be regarded as an ego trip to make me look important at your expense (3). As Mr Coxwell is the Company Secretary, we have come appropriately dressed for a board meeting. Not too smart – ruffled shirts and flashy ties are out! Wear a dark suit and if you can find a waistcoat, so much the better. In my experience, only about 95 per cent of company secretaries wear this type of uniform, so you could meet the only Elton John type of company secretary in the country and look hopelessly out of place. Take the odds (3).

Then take Mr Coxwell's coat. 'Before we go into lunch, Mr Coxwell, may I suggest that you see the Ballroom first, so that you know the setting.' 'Before we go into lunch' will reassure him that he is going to get some; he hasn't made a mistake about that either (3)!' 'May I suggest' – nobody is going to order him about (3). 'The setting' because it is important to Mr Coxwell and not just an area where each guest will take on 1500 calories (1).

We will have made sure that the lights are turned on in the room so that we don't have to go groping around in the dark, and we have our book of photographs, floor plans and menu dishes to hand because the room is not at present set up (2).

Mr Coxwell walks beside me to the Ballroom. I do not lead the way, like Dr Livingstone, with the bearers bringing up the rear (3). If there is not room for two abreast, then I say 'Shall I lead on?' but only until the corridor widens and I can fall back in line with Mr Coxwell (3).

When we reach the Ballroom, Mr Coxwell is ushered in first. If the room is tight for 150, we keep walking, and therefore so does Mr Coxwell, until we have reached a corner. Then we turn and Mr Coxwell sees the room at its largest. If you stop in the middle of the room, the client can only see the size by turning his eyes in a full circle, and it is difficult to gauge size accurately that way. If Mr Coxwell decides at this point that the room is too small, we probably have an insoluble problem on our hands. We have to persuade him that he is wrong, and you must try never to get into that position at any time because people don't like to admit they are wrong. In the corner we have the best chance. If, on the other hand, the room takes 300 and Mr Coxwell is likely to think that his party will be swamped, then we stand in the middle of the room and it looks that much smaller. You and I both know that there are many ways of making a room appear smaller if necessary; set the tables further apart, put in serving tables, a bigger stage; it is not difficult. But Mr Coxwell might not know that, so in that situation we stand in the middle of the room.

Now there are two of us and only one of Mr Coxwell, and I'm over 6 feet tall and a tiny bit overweight. We don't want Mr Coxwell to feel boxed in by our physical bulk – well mine anyway. So we don't line up on either side of him. Instead, you stand to my side, away from Mr Coxwell, and he stands nearer the door. The escape route is open. If he is short, then we stand a little further away so that our height and bulk is reduced by the distance. Mr Coxwell feels quite safe (3). Far fetched? Try putting yourself in a room between a young lady and the door and see; or tower over a child or a dog and observe their reaction.

'Mr Coxwell, this room is 60 feet long by 45 feet wide and it can comfortably take 150 guests' (2). Everybody likes the sound of their own name, so we use it quite frequently (3). Be careful here; I once had a client, named Robinson shall we say, who had been a regular in the Indian Army before he retired and went to work for a large association. He was a very nice man, Major Robinson, but although we knew each other for some years, I never did achieve a very good rapport with him. I mentioned this to his successor. 'He was a very pleasant man, your predecessor,' I said, 'but I always found Major Robinson a bit distant.' The new client looked at me like my old Headmaster. 'Derek' he said, 'do you mean Major-General Robinson?' Do be sure to get the name right.

Know the dimensions of your rooms – in metres as well as in feet nowadays, but the former won't mean much to anybody under 40 even now. Feet and inches mean nothing to anybody under 15 – the next generation of clients – so learn both. Here you are establishing that the room can take the numbers because you obviously worked it out carefully (2).

'This is a fairly elaborate dinner,' Mr Coxwell says. 'We sometimes bring in displays.' Mr Coxwell had no difficulty in interrupting my description of the room. You always watch the client's mouth. If it opens, you stop – in full flow if necessary – so that the client can say what he wants. You are telling your side of the story about the product. The client has to marry that information with what he wants to buy. It is no use prattling on about the air conditioning if he is still wondering about the seating plan you have just outlined. When a client interrupts, he is starting to buy, beginning the marrying-up process. Encourage that tiny buying bud to grow; do not drown it in a sea of additional information before it is ready to absorb some more moisture. Not to be able to interrupt irritates clients. Don't put them in that position (3). I have a friend who is a hotel manager of the old school, and when he talks, his staff listen politely. He expects the clients to do the same and if they try to interrupt, he simply raises his voice and stops them. Not a method to be recommended!

'You can bring in the displays from the street, Mr Coxwell. The entrance door is 11 feet high and 14 feet wide and the floor is reinforced. Dere, you looked after that car launch last week, didn't you?'

The size of the entrance door establishes professional knowledge again (2). The car launch established that the floor really is reinforced (2) and this, in its

46

turn, starts to establish credibility. Mr Coxwell has to be persuaded that he can believe us. Saying it can be done is not the same as proving it. Build credibility by proof wherever possible.

Now notice that you have emerged at this point. Not as Mr Reader, but as Dere. And you are going to be calling me Derek. Mr Coxwell can hardly object to the mode of address between colleagues, but it puts him slightly outside the party. There's Dere and Derek and Mr Coxwell. As the lunch goes on – yes, I know we haven't even got near the restaurant yet; be patient – Mr Coxwell is likely to feel secure enough and enjoying the company enough to say, 'Why don't you call me Bob?' In establishing a rapport, this would obviously be a move in the right direction.

There is another way; if you have two clients to lunch and you are already on first-name terms with one of them, the second is almost bound to fall into line. 'Mr Coxwell, this is John Lyning, Managing Director of Mayfair Flintknapping. John, this is . . . I'm sorry Mr Coxwell, I don't know your first name?' John will now call him Bob, or the lunch will continue between John, Derek and Mr Coxwell until Mr Coxwell says, 'Call me Bob'. Which he will, unless he is the last of the very old school. The importance of the rapport is obvious. The barrier is not usually put up by the client but by the hotel executive. It is the hotelier who sets up the iron curtain of formal dress, formal relationships – 'Good morning, sir' – and formal communications. The client is not usually the problem, but let it be crystal clear that it is only the client's decision whether to call you by your first name. You never use his first name until he has made that decision in your favour (3).

All things being equal, if Mr Coxwell has to decide between a letter from the Splendide, a meeting with Mr Formaliti, the Banqueting Manager at the Regency Grand, or lunch with Derek and Dere, you are home and dry.

To any good salesman, the responsibility of looking after the client is a heavy one. It isn't just that you have persuaded this man to give you the business and therefore have an obligation not to let him down. It is also the fact that if you do let him down, you don't get his business next time, and have to find someone else to take his place – which is tiresome if you are trying to improve on last year's figures. So even if you have so arranged the conversation that you finish on first-name terms, this in no way reduces your responsibility to the client. Indeed, the more friendly the relationship, the more responsibility you feel. Let it also be said that with the professional buyer, first-name terms do not advance your case one scrap.

We left Mr Coxwell asking about how to get displays into the room. When selling a dinner, the question of displays would not normally come up until very late in the conversation. But it is important to Mr Coxwell, so it is dealt with straight away. A sales presentation must be absolutely flexible. I have seen salesmen who have been trained to start on page 1 of the company presentation manual and go through to page 73 like parrots. If you stop them at page 22 to ask a question out of context, they don't know the answer, and have to go back to page 1 to pick up the thread at the beginning. An extreme example maybe, but it does occur; it must not happen to us (2).

The subject of displays being unusual, the salesman's mental antenna should quiver. Why is that important? Now everybody buys things for differ-ent reasons. You might buy a particular car as a means of getting from A to B; as a way of impressing a girl-friend; as a status symbol; or to irritate your father who always said you would never earn enough to be able to afford one. People buy banquets for different reasons too, and the difficulty is to find out what is the important factor or factors to them. Mr Coxwell has talked about displays too early in the normal process. If it is that important, we should home in on that point; displays after all are not one of our weaknesses. 'How large are your displays usually, Mr Coxwell?'

Not, 'Why on earth do you bring in displays for a dinner?' Too inquisitive, too nosy and rude: just drum up some more conversation about displays. 'They can be very big. The Chairman likes to demonstrate the Company's progress to the executives after dinner.'

Information is flooding in. It is the Chairman's dinner. We couldn't get more than 'a dinner for senior management' out of Mr Coxwell when we first telephoned; also Mr Coxwell apparently worries about pleasing his Chairman. The Chairman likes the displays and the Chairman's likes come first. Mr Coxwell did not ask 'Where are the kitchens?', to ascertain that the food will be hot, or where the reception will be held, because the fellows like plenty of room to have a drink. No, it is the displays that are important, because the Chairman matters. Not all chairmen do; some are figureheads. Mr Coxwell's isn't; it is short odds that he's a dragon! But we're a long way from the finishing line.

'I see'. That phrase and, 'I understand', are important, the client seldom says 'Now make a note of that, because it's important'. He emphasises certain points and wants them picked up by the salesman. He doesn't want to say his Chairman is a holy terror if things go wrong, but he wants the message understood. 'I see' (1) and a note on the little pad we are, of course, carrying makes the point. The notebook is essential. It can be a piece of paper, and I have been guilty of writing on them in the past, but a notebook looks much more professional (2). 'Well, you'll have noticed that we have 16 spotlights in the ceiling, which can be adjusted to light and display. They are controlled from that panel of switches over there' (2).

'Well, you'll have noticed,' tells him to look. Imparting information to a client must be done tactfully. The likelihood is that he won't have noticed; after all he has only just got into the room. But we give him credit for noticing. Just as we say 'as you know' before telling him things he is very likely not to know. 'As you know, the wines from the Avignon region, such as *Chateauneuf du Pape*, are rather stronger than the clarets'. No, he probably doesn't know; but we cannot be accused of teaching him, because we say 'as you know'. We are merely confirming knowledge he is already deemed to have: much more courteous (3).

'Do you have a lot of other important speeches, as well as the Chairman's?' The point we are trying to establish is whether we have to influence other people as well. If it's a one-man show, then only one man can be upset.

'The Finance Director and the Sales and Production Directors give resumés of their departments as well,' says Mr Coxwell, 'but the main speech is, of course, that of the Chairman.'

Now we need to find out whether this is the high spot of the evening, or just one part of the proceedings. It might be possible to home in on the excellence of our sound equipment and get away with the fact that the dance floor is a bit tight for 150.

'Do you invite the ladies as well?'

Notice, 'ladies': it is a small courtesy, but it is a pleasant compliment to Mr Coxwell's firm (3).

'No, not on this occasion. We usually have a party at the Chairman's home in the Spring for the ladies.'

You make a note in the book to check out the accommodation the visiting couples might need in the Spring, but you don't switch to that subject yet. One thing at a time. The information is written down; it won't run away. We now know that it is an all-male gathering for a state-of-the-nation briefing for the senior management of the company; a Chairman's dinner with all the top brass in attendance on a three-line whip. Small sigh of relief that we don't need to worry about the dance floor! It would be logical at this point to assume that money is no object and only the best need be mentioned. Professional salesmen are more cautious than that.

'Have you set a budget for the cost of the evening, Mr Coxwell?' We could have asked what Mr Coxwell wants to spend on the whole evening. The danger with that approach is that Mr Coxwell might not want to tell us. A professional buyer doesn't tell you what he wants to pay; he waits for you to name a price first. We don't want to do that because we might be quoting too low. So, to obtain the maximum information, we ask the question in two parts; is there a budget, and then what is the budget?

'Oh yes,' says Mr Coxwell. 'The Chairman is always anxious that the top management set a good example. He feels that to ask everybody else to work within a budget and then to allow the Chairman's dinner to cost the earth would be quite wrong.'

You could at this point take the part of the senior management. You could point out that they do the most work and never get paid overtime, that to be miserly with them is penny wise and pound foolish, and say that you wouldn't want to work for a lot of mean skinflints like Canwe, Seldom & Co. This would be extremely foolish, as Mr Coxwell is in no position to change the policy. And if you criticise his Chairman now, then (thinks!) maybe you will pour soup over him at the function! The objective is to get the business, not to act as shop steward for the directors.

'Yes, of course,' is as far as you go, in a non-committal voice. Your voice must be a highly flexible weapon. It must be under control at all times. 'Yes, of course,' in a 'nudge, nudge, wink, wink' sort of voice could ruin the whole sale at this point. The game must be played straight, even if you know that the Chairman of Canwe, Seldom has been keeping a mistress in the company flat at the company's expense for years, because it's even been in the gossip columns. You could further prove your discretion with the right inflexion (1, 2, 3).

'What would you like the budget to cover?'

Notice that we have not got hung up on the cost of the menu. Most clients feel that the only way they can judge what the whole function will cost is by finding out the menu price. If they don't like the minimum price they go elsewhere. No, we will decide what the menu costs when we know first what the budget covers, and then how large it is.

'Let me see,' said Mr Coxwell, 'it should cover the drinks before dinner, the menu, naturally, a choice of claret or a hock, liqueurs and cigars of course, and then we usually have a few decanters of port as well.'

Never take what a client says at face value. They are not supposed to be experts at hotel banqueting and they usually forget something. We soon establish that Mr Coxwell also wants the budget to include cigarettes on the table, menu printing, flowers, service, VAT and a number of bottles of champagne, which the company provided, and which were to be handed by the Chairman to each executive as a memento of a good year (2). You write it all down, doing the figure work in your head if you possibly can.

'A four-course dinner? Or five courses?'

'Yes, five normally. We don't have a cabaret, so the meal doesn't have to be completed in a mad rush.'

There is a grey area here. Is the eating and drinking so leisurely that the speeches are said to be important but really aren't? At the moment though we need the budget figure, so we haven't time to check the importance of that last remark, yet. But we keep it in mind. 'One hundred and fifty guests,' I repeat. 'What . . . about £3,000?'

At this specific point you look straight at the client. You have been looking at your figures and now you gaze at him. You thereby convey that you have nothing to be ashamed of as far as your price is concerned. You are not hanging your head or averting your gaze and you can see his reaction: disapproval, maybe with accompanying frown, crossed arms, a shift backwards; or approval, with possible smile, air of relaxation, no worried look in the eyes. At this early stage of the meeting, before lunch, it is going to worry him if the price is way out of the budget. He still has to get through another hour with you and the atmosphere, he expects will tend to cool if you find that there is no way of doing business.

The £3,000 is not a guess. You need to know the approximate prices of everything he wants included. Jot them down, add up for each guest, and multiply by 150. Professional salesmen should have no need for calculators. The use of a calculator obviously must warn the customer that you are working out the figures and there is always the impression given that you are checking up on him to see if he has got his sums wrong. The right impression is that you have selected a rough figure after a little casual conversation and by a lucky chance it happens to be about right. Equally if it happens to be wrong, then it was just a casual shot in the dark, and you can – on reflection – see the error of your ways and adjust it accordingly when he says so. Or if he says so. But Mr Coxwell says 'About £3,000,' with a slight smile. Mr Coxwell knows something about buying and knows that he shouldn't divulge his budget so that the salesman has more reason to reduce prices to get within it. We have a counter to this however, because we know now that there is something more important to Mr Coxwell than getting a cut price.

'It is obviously particularly important to keep within the budget, Mr Coxwell, as it's the Chairman who wants to set a good example. He certainly wouldn't like to acknowledge that the final bill was way over the agreed figure. But a lot of clients feel that they are at a disadvantage with a hotel, because we're spending your money. When we pour the drinks for example. You might find yourself over budget with little you can do about it. It has therefore always seemed important to us to take on the responsibility for ensuring that you keep strictly within your budget by doing the monitoring very carefully throughout the evening' (2).

All this has been said in a fluent passage. There have been no pauses for Mr Coxwell to interrupt, because it is important to put that argument in one piece. When you say, for instance, that a client might feel at a disadvantage, you don't want to have Mr Coxwell contradict you before you have explained why this is the case. You also have made the adverse results of overspending a little more melodramatic than might be justified. 'Way over', 'strictly within', 'monitoring very carefully' are all slight exaggerations, but they do leave the client with the clear understanding that you take this question very seriously. He doesn't want to admit that he is scared of facing the Chairman with a bill that is too high, but you have said it for him, in so many words.

'I have always been told by other hotels that you can't estimate drink consumption,' Mr Coxwell comments.

It is perfectly true that a lot of hotels do say this. It is an excellent excuse for three shortcomings: first, to steal from the client by padding his bill with the cost of drinks he hasn't had; second, to get him to spend more than he wanted, on the highly questionable theory that it is better to get more money from him today than the possibility of more business from him tomorrow; and third, that it is far easier not even to try to keep within his budget because it takes less work. The truth is that it is perfectly easy to estimate expenditure in advance and stick to it. The great danger in suggesting otherwise is that a good salesman is going to come along from another organisation and tell the client what can be done if one tries. The client then realises that his original hotel has led him up the garden path, and their credibility is sadly dented. He remembers all those occasions when he has felt that he was overcharged, and now he knows it wasn't necessary. The resulting anger, of course, is not directed at you but at the competition.

'No, it's quite simple really.' And you go on to explain how it is done. Notice that you have contradicted him; you said 'no', and you never contradict a client *unless* he is merely repeating the opinion of someone else. If Mr Coxwell had said 'I don't think . . .' then your reply would have been, 'That's very understandable. It is difficult, but' (3).

We have now reassured Mr Coxwell about the budget and that the room is large enough for his purpose. We can probably now leave, but not before asking, 'Is there anything else I can tell you about the room?' There is always a need to continue checking that the client isn't keeping a question or two up his sleeve rather than 'bother' you with details.

'It's quite a high ceiling,' says Mr Coxwell. 'Will everybody be able to hear all right?'

Good; now you can settle the problem in his mind instead of having him fret about it. You explain the microphone system and the advantages of halter microphones over standing ones. The halter microphone goes round the neck of the speaker, who doesn't have to do anything to help it pick up his voice. The standing microphone either restricts the speaker to gazing at the thing, or, if he ignores it and turns away, his voice ebbs and flows like the tide. Not helpful if the speaker is trying to put over something important. You clear all this with Mr Coxwell (1 and 2).

Then when you have proved to Mr Coxwell's satisfaction the effectiveness of your amplification, you make a virtue of the high ceiling.

'Of course, you'd be absolutely right that without decent amplification, a high ceiling can make the speeches very difficult to hear. But if the microphones are good, a high ceiling does have one great advantage. There is bound to be a lot of conversation and the acoustics ensure that the noise level remains reasonably low. I have always found this very important because it gets more difficult as the years go by to distinguish one voice from another in a crowd' (2).

This is absolutely true but it is a point very often ignored by young people. They do not realise the irritation of trying to distinguish what is being said to you at a cocktail party, when the various conversations make it impossible to tell one voice from another. You might well find that Mr Coxwell agrees entirely because he has the same problem; finding small points you have in common also helps to build the relationship.

'Of course, it's always difficult to visualise a room set up the way we want it,' says Mr Coxwell.

'Well, I haven't got a photograph of it precisely as it would be, Mr Coxwell, but I can give you a pretty good idea.' And we show the appropriate photograph in the presentation book, and from the floor plan indicate the microphone points. Exactly when you use a presentation book depends on how well the sale is going. It is a very powerful weapon for the salesman because it provides incontrovertible evidence and, as such, it is best on most occasions to keep it in reserve for times when you run into trouble.

Now usher the client ahead of us this time, with you and me bringing up the rear (3) and making a quick mental check: what have we still to learn? We have that grey area about the leisurely meal, which brought into question the real importance of the speeches. And we need to know who organises the Chairman's party at his home in the Spring, so that we can try to get the overnight accommodation.

Let us pause here for a moment and review the sales presentation so far. The first thing to notice is that we have discussed very little which is of interest to the hotel banqueting department. We haven't talked about the menu, the timing, the drinks, the seating plan or arrangements for the bar after dinner. We have only talked about those points which are most important to Mr Coxwell. If, under that heading, had come the question of menus or drinks, then we would have tackled those points first, but the presentation is carried out in terms of the client's priorities and not in some predetermined form set down by the Banqueting Enquiry Sheet.

The second thing to notice is that each word the professional salesman uses is checked carefully before it is uttered. This demands intense concentration and very quick thinking. Nothing is said carelessly; the possible areas of misinterpretation by the client are examined in advance so that there should be no reason for misunderstanding. The presentation may sound casual but it is, in fact, most carefully orchestrated. It would be unreasonable to judge yourself too harshly if you failed to achieve that standard in the early days of selling. The important thing to recognise is what you eventually want to achieve.

How to Sell Banquets

We are now seated in the bar, Mr Coxwell has his drink, and we can start again. The presentation is under our control. We must gently direct it in the way we want it to go, by bringing up the subjects and asking the questions. This is not in any way to contradict the statement that we must deal with the client's priorities first if we can. You ask questions to find the priorities, and then deal with them.

'Spending about £3,000 on one evening is a lot of money, Mr Coxwell. What are you particularly trying to achieve?' (1) Note that we are not pretending that £3,000 is just a drop in the ocean; we are showing a proper regard for the customer's investment. I have said 'about' because I don't want to deal with any price haggling until I know a lot more about the dinner.

'I suppose it has two purposes really,' says Mr Coxwell, 'we're saying "thank you" to the senior men for all their efforts over the year, and we're encouraging them to do a lot better during the next year.'

'So you want the dinner to be memorable in itself as a high point in the company year' (1).

'Within the budget,' says Mr Coxwell firmly.

We have now established that the dinner is not a question of providing 1500 calories. A lot of meals we serve in hotels under the heading of banqueting are really just that. It applies to a number of the conferences, the dances and the dinners with important speakers. This one is not in that category.

'What have you served in the past, Mr Coxwell?' (1) Ostensibly this seems to be a question designed to avoid serving the same dishes again. In reality, it is to establish what proved unacceptable or unattractive in the past. Suppose that Mr Coxwell can't stand chicken as a main course. Without some sort of clue, you might suggest it or other dishes he dislikes, and this sets up resistance. You are trying at all times not to say something which Mr Coxwell finds it necessary to contradict. You want the client to say 'yes' all the time so that – and this you may find difficult to believe – when it comes to the question of whether he will take the hotel, he is more inclined to say 'yes' to that as well. It *is* a fact that if the client starts to get into a 'no' phase in dealing with you, he has to be coaxed out of it before he is asked for the business

'Over the years, I suppose we've tried most things,' says Mr Coxwell. 'Chicken, duck, lamb, steak. I know it isn't easy to cater for large numbers.'

Customers often say something of this sort and it is an oblique way of criticising standards they have found wanting in the past. As he is your guest, the client does not want to be abrasive in criticising the industry, but he still isn't happy with the way things have gone in the past. After all, why should he be shopping at all if the last hotel looked after him well? We examine this last point more carefully.

'Do you usually go to a different hotel each year for the dinner?'

'No, we've been to the last place for three years now, and we thought we might have a change.'

You would have been happier to hear that last year was the first time and a disaster, but at least a desire for a change is helpful.

'Was it becoming a bit repetitive?' We must find out what the hotel did wrong.

'I'll be honest,' says Mr Coxwell. 'All my experience with hotels is that they make a great effort when you first go to them and then the standard of attention drops as the years go by.'

Now are we going to defend the industry at this point? Are we going to point out the difficulties in coming up with new ideas every year? No, we are not.

'Stupid, isn't it?' I comment. 'After all, it should be much easier to look after a client whose likes and dislikes you know than a relative stranger.' Not a complete stranger. You have only just met Mr Coxwell himself. 'A lot of friends say the same thing.' Friends, not clients, establishes the relationship you enjoy with others.

'We've been looking after Harry Brown of Unichem for twelve years now, so I get a lot of opportunity to talk to him about the situation round the country. He books conferences and dinners pretty regularly, and he confirms exactly the same thing.'

Yes, you agree with him, but you bring a client to your defence who would confirm that it doesn't happen here. Try to produce a non-contentious multi-national company in case the client has prejudices you might upset; mentioning a famous German firm will not help if your client had a close relative who died in the war, and the Christian name further establishes the good relationship.

'There is, in fact, no way of proving that this hotel is any different, Mr Coxwell. The proof of the pudding would be in the eating' (3).

Having brought in your witness, you then admit that you can't disprove the criticism 100 per cent. It is very important not even to try to prove your hotel innocent of every criticism; to try to prove that you have the perfect product, the right size, the right decor, the right equipment, the right price, the right everything. There just aren't any products in the whole world which are perfect, and any attempt to show your hotel in that light is bound to create a credibility gap. The impression you want to give the client is that you are more often right than wrong, and a small margin better than any competitor. I always use a story to illustrate this question of the impossibility of perfection. It is about the first night of *The Doctor's Dilemma*. It appears that the curtain finally fell to rapturous applause and calls for the author. So Bernard Shaw eventually went on stage to make a curtain speech, but the applause went on and on. Eventually it died down and finally there was complete silence in the auditorium. So Shaw stepped forward to convey his thanks. Before he could start, in the complete hush, there came one enormous 'Boo' from the gallery. Shaw looked up and said, 'I quite agree, sir. But who are we two amongst so many?' Probably apocryphal, but very much to the point. If you use a similar story to show the client you don't think you are perfect, he will not immediately seek another hotel from sheer disappointment. The British dislike boasting at the best of times and the experienced client knows that he has to choose the lesser of the many evils (3). 'The proof of the pudding would be in the eating.' A small and innocuous play on words: an inoffensive witticism, but one which establishes that you are not a robot activated only by business. You can joke about your own industry, and you do realise that you are in a fun occupation.

When Mr Coxwell complains about hotels being less attentive as years go by, you could have said you wouldn't be like that, but he wouldn't have believed you. Now you can investigate what went wrong with the last hotel.

'What particular aspects seem to slacken off?' Not, how did the last hotel foul you up, because that is too direct. The answer to the question you asked will bring it out just as well.

'It's the little things that go wrong. They forget that the Chairman likes Bailey's Irish Cream. Or they don't bring the fresh coffee I always order to be put on the table just before the speeches start, so that people can help themselves. Or they clatter in the kitchen during the speeches, so that I have to go out and ask them to be quiet. That sort of thing.'

It is the speeches which are top of Mr Coxwell's worries. That grey area is black and white now.

We talk about putting the Head Waiter on guard to keep things quiet, of making detailed notes of all the small points and confirming them (1). Then we go back to the subject of the menu, which you will remember we left when Mr Coxwell raised the point about hotels slackening off.

'You know, Mr Coxwell, if you have 150 guests to dinner, it is almost impossible to produce a menu that everybody likes. On the vegetables alone, there is bound to be somebody who can't stand the choice.' Notice that it is 'the choice' and not 'your choice'. Mr Coxwell will be making the decision, but no criticism attaches to 'the choice' (3).

'Within reason, there are two things you can do. You can either have a menu the Chairman is going to enjoy, or preferably one that both you and the Chairman will enjoy. After all, you are the one who is going to be doing all the work.'

Perhaps for the first time, someone has acknowledged that Mr Coxwell, in addition to his heavy duties as Company Secretary, also has to shoulder the burden of this additional chore, for which, if he is lucky, he may get a pat on the back; but if it goes wrong, he will never hear the end of it. You are verbally clapping Mr Coxwell who has been waiting a long time for the applause he feels he richly deserves (3).

'I suppose I like veal best of all,' says Mr Coxwell, 'but you can hardly serve 150 *Escalope Viennoise.*'

'It is certainly better in a sauce if you want it piping hot I agree, but we could try one of the Chef's specialities, *Piccata de Veau au Marsala.* You know, the small fillets in a Marsala wine sauce' (2).

Now the possibility exists that the chef does not have *Piccata* in his repertoire, which would be unlucky as he'd have to learn it for Mr Coxwell. You must differentiate between levels of difficulty. It is impossible to serve Mixed Grill adequately for 150, so the salesman doesn't sell that. If a dish is possible, though, there is plenty of time for the kitchen to brush up on it before the banquet takes place.

It is time to start a new tack. But first is Mr Coxwell enjoying himself? He has been seated in the bar so that he isn't boxed in in a corner by you and me; the bar-tender has brought him the drink he ordered, and did not fail to wipe the bottom of the glass, so that Mr Coxwell's tie does not get drips on it when he picks up the aperitif. That's all satisfactory. At all times we are working on these two entirely separate planes; to sell the banquet, and to ensure that the client is not going to have his visit to the hotel spoiled by shortcomings on the part of any member of the staff.

The tack we choose at this point is the creation of particular ideas which are going to make Mr Coxwell look efficient in the eyes of his Chairman. These will be in the presentation of the banquet and they will distinguish us from the hotel down the road which will not be equally imaginative. Watch how this works.

'Mr Coxwell, one of the areas of expertise you are paying for when you use a hotel is our ability to put over your company's message in the menu. To take a simple example, it is very easy to put pasta 'C's and 'S's in a consommé for Canwe, Seldom.'

'Nice touch,' says Mr Coxwell.

If he had said that he had used the idea before, we could have assessed how novel we had to be, but it seems to be quite new to him. The creativity born of chefs like Carême, Soyer and Escoffier seems to have been flagging in recent years. . . . 'What was the keynote of the Chairman's message last year?'

'Five million pounds profit,' says Mr Coxwell promptly.

'Well, let's select the right creative idea. Suppose last year, after the dessert, we had served macaroons instead of *petit fours*, with coffee – which would have helped your budget. On the base of the macaroons is rice paper, as you know, and in vegetable ink on that rice paper we could have stamped the figures £5,000,000.'

How to Sell Banquets

By this point, Mr Coxwell doesn't have the faintest idea where you are leading him. Gastronomically he is already well out of his depth with rice paper and vegetable inks (2). You come to the denouement. 'The guests would have seen the figures on the rice paper, and when the Chairman makes his speech and asks for £5 million profit, he takes one of the macaroons and says, "And I hope that this is the last time I shall have to eat my own words" (1).'

It is a good line for a speech. It is simple, it shows forethought, you can't see the punchline coming and it sticks in the mind afterwards, which is what the speaker wants to achieve. And how will Mr Coxwell present it to his Chairman in conversation? Will he give the hotel the credit? It isn't very likely. He will probably say that he was discussing the function with the hotel and he got this good idea. And this is what you want him to do. Why don't you want the credit for the hotel? Because Mr Coxwell himself knows where the idea came from, and if this year's banquet is a success, next year the Chairman will want some more good ideas, and where is Mr Coxwell going to get them? From you, which is one of the most powerful reasons for coming back.

Once the client begins to appreciate what can be done with creative ideas – dismissed as gimmicks, but they are really good memory joggers and image builders – you can take him through the whole gamut. Company colours reproduced in the flower arrangements, rolls in the shape of 'C's and 'S's, all the areas we cover in the chapter on creative banqueting.

Early on, however, you point out two things to Mr Coxwell. First, that these ideas are not necessarily expensive – the macaroons being cheaper than the *petit fours* is a good start – and second that they are only suggestions, and there are plenty more if he doesn't like those you produce at the beginning. You want Mr Coxwell to look at the ideas without the worry that he might be buying something more expensive or that he is imposing on you by asking for more ideas. It is useful if you can go into lunch after establishing the value of gimmicks, but before the range has been more than touched upon. It gives you a good topic to discuss whilst waiting for the first course.

Your priority now is to take a quick look round the dining-table to ensure that Mr Coxwell has everything he needs, then you can carry on with the gimmicks. As Mr Coxwell agrees to the individual ideas, he is still not saying you can have the business, but he is putting a lot of his own time and effort into the banquet with you at this point. It isn't just a question of getting sample menus. He is building this function brick by brick even if, eventually, another hotel is selected, when all the plans you are putting together may well be wasted. But you are helping with the building and that is why it is so silly to spend entertaining time on social chit-chat. That doesn't add anything to Mr Coxwell's in-put on the function and therefore it doesn't help you to get it.

We must continue to build on that foundation of work. The gimmicks are in there, we have established in many ways the commitment and expertise. Where can we go now? Well, we can tackle that bugbear of Mr Coxwell's – the budget.

'Mr Coxwell, we've agreed that one thing the Chairman particularly wants is to stay within the budget. Obviously a great deal of the responsibility for that falls on us.' Mr Coxwell is surprised. He is accustomed to hotels trying to shift that responsibility away from themselves. There are all too many clients who plan to spend £500 and finish up spending £600. This may be because they were cheated, but it is usually because they were ill-advised about their likely expenditure, or alternatively that the hotel did not keep a proper control over the evening.

Let us examine this a little more closely. To be cheated is simply to be charged for cocktails you didn't consume, cigars you didn't smoke, and wine that wasn't poured. Many many years ago I was watching a function because I was so pleased to have sold it, and the manager invited me to dinner. It was a very good dinner, and the wine was magnificent – a Corton 1937. I offered to pay for my share, but the manager said this wasn't necessary as it would be put on the bill of my banqueting client the next morning. I wanted that client back, and he had trusted me when I told him I would look after him. So, in a fine temper, I told my superior the next morning what I thought of the hotel industry's traditions. He calmed me down, agreed that it was disgraceful, and promised to see that it never happened again. I was mollified, and only found out some years later that what he had actually done was to call in the Manager and tell him that if he wanted to rob the guests, would he please ensure that I wasn't told, as I had some very odd views on the subject!

If the client is ill-advised about expenditure, he is simply allowed to dig his own budgetary grave. He assumes too low a spending level and the hotel allows him to work on this assumption in order to get the business. This isn't robbery but it also isn't customer service. The client is entitled to be displeased when the bill comes in, loaded with extras. A lack of control has the same effect as a lack of advice. Dinner announced after cocktails have been served for 45 minutes instead of half an hour inevitably puts up the bill the client expects to receive. So does pouring large measures, topping up wine glasses unnecessarily, and many other tricks of the trade. It can be carelessness and it can be sharp practice to manufacture a larger bill. If it results in the client getting too large a bill and swearing never to come back again, it serves the hotel right. If the client also tells his friends not to use you, that is a just punishment as well. Our job is to protect the client from his own lack of knowledge.

'I've always been told that there isn't a lot an hotel can do to ensure that we keep to the budget,' said Mr Coxwell. 'How do you manage it?'

'Suppose we divide the expenditure into the items of which we know the

-exact cost and those we have to control on the night. We know the cost of the menu, the menu printing, flowers, light refreshments before the end of the evening if you want them, and cigarettes on the tables.'

'Yes, I can see that, but there are still many other items, mostly in the way of drinks.'

'Exactly, so the first area is cocktails before dinner. Now there are two ways of overspending a budget on cocktails. It is reasonable to expect that guests will, on average, have a drink every ten minutes. So if you allow half an hour for cocktails, you can estimate three drinks for each guest. But as everybody won't arrive at the beginning, two and a half is a fairer guess. Now the two ways of overspending are to have the cocktail time go beyond 30 minutes, or to put more than a measure in the glass. If we announce dinner promptly, the time for drinking won't allow for excessive expenditure. If we measure the drinks, you won't get charged for doubles' (2).

'Two and a half drinks doesn't seem unreasonable,' says Mr Coxwell, 'Is there in fact any other way of reducing expenditure?'

You want Mr Coxwell back in subsequent years. Educating him is a good long-term investment, even if it may cost you a little turnover in year one. You tell him.

'There is one other way. Guests can't drink cocktails until they actually get into the room. They can't get into the room if there's a queue. So if the Chairman shakes everybody's hand and talks to them when they arrive, it will not only be a gracious way of receiving the guests, it will also reduce the expenditure on cocktails' (2).

Mr Coxwell laughs. 'I never thought of that,' he says. 'I must tell the Chairman. But I think he'll let them get into the room.'

An extra good mark for Mr Coxwell when he tells the Chairman. You have shown him a new way to reduce expenditure which illustrates that you are on his side, and he hasn't taken you up on it, so you can have your cake and eat it.

'The next area we have to control,' we continue, 'is wine consumption. Now you get six glasses to a bottle and the largest area of waste is the wine left in the glass. Most people have a preference for either sweet or dry wine, and will drink little of the one they like less. So if you have both white and red, one or other will tend to get left. I know that white wine should be drunk with fish and red wine with meat, but you can't force a guest to drink what he doesn't enjoy. The cheapest way of serving wine is to offer a choice of either red or white.'

'I accept that,' says Mr Coxwell. 'In fact, the white Burgundies give me a lot of indigestion now that I'm not as young as I was. But the Chairman is a stickler for convention in these matters, so I expect we'll have both.'

'All right. Then the next best way to reduce expenditure is to agree in advance that the white wine with the fish course will not be topped up. We'll

60

serve one glass, and then we'll serve the red wine with the main course.'

'Yes, that seems eminently reasonable,' agrees Mr Coxwell.

'So we know the cost of the white wine: 150 guests, 6 glasses to a bottle, 25 bottles. On the same basis we can say one and a half glasses of the red wine, which allows one topping up before we reach the coffee and liqueurs. Now you have seen your guests at these parties before. What percentage of them would you say take a liqueur and a cigar?'

'I suppose about three-quarters of them will take a liqueur, but I don't expect more than half of them will have a cigar. The trouble with cigars is that they do tend to get left, half smoked in the ash trays. When I think of the cost of them nowadays, I hate to see such waste.'

'I agree, if you're serving Havanas, one has to be a regular cigar smoker to appreciate them. Let a Havana go out and try to relight it, and it can become very pungent. It really is better with guests who don't regularly smoke cigars, to give them something milder like a Jamaican with a Cameroons wrapper. The Royal Jamaican are cheaper than the Havanas and really very good. Why not offer a choice of one or the other? (2)'

'Yes, good idea,' says Mr Coxwell. 'They can always take a Havana if they want one.'

It is important that the banquet salesman knows all his products, not just the food or the wine. It is a fact that the consumption of Havana cigars in this country has slumped from around 75,000,000 at the turn of the century to about 10,000,000 today. It isn't the price, because they were always expensive; it is the lack of knowledge about how to get the best enjoyment from them.

'So now we can estimate the consumption of drinks before dinner, wine, liqueurs and cigars with dinner. What arrangements do you make after dinner is over?'

'We have decanters of port on the table and let that suffice. Otherwise the speeches get interrupted by the waiter service.'

'That certainly makes it easier to estimate the cost of drinks after dinner. If you have a free bar, it is the one area which you cannot estimate, but if you allow two or three glasses of port maximum, you should be quite safe.'

'What can you do to stop the bar after dinner going way over the budget?' asked Mr Coxwell. 'We do have one on occasions for other functions.'

Make a note on your pad about other functions. We'll dig into those later, but for the moment just answer the question.

'The best way is to stock a bar with the amount which has been agreed for drinks after dinner, and then tell the organiser when it is exhausted. He can then either agree to a further supply or close the bar. At least in that way you have the opportunity to stop expenditure instead of just being faced with a bill at the end of the banquet.'

'Then why,' Mr Coxwell asks, 'do hotels tell me that they can't estimate my bill in advance?'

That's the $64,000 question and there are many ways of burying the competition at this point. To be too critical, however, is to boast of your own ability by contrast.

'I don't honestly know, Mr Coxwell. As you can see, it really isn't that difficult' (3). And leave the client to work it out for himself.

At this point Mr Coxwell starts to do some sums in his own notebook and finally says, 'Well, you're not at all bad on price, and I like the room. You're sure the sound equipment is first-rate?'

'Yes, I wouldn't let you down' (1). It helps at some point to actually put that sentiment into words. You wouldn't let the client down and you can tell him so.

'Oh, I'm sure you wouldn't,' says Mr Coxwell who, if he is a sensible man, has still to be totally convinced. You never know if a supplier is really going to do a good job until you have given him a job to do. The client knows that as well.

We have now reached a crucial point. As far as we can see there was nothing wrong with the room, we've discussed the budget and the menu and still found no insuperable problems. This is the point where the amateur salesman does one of two things; he either starts talking socially about subjects quite unconnected with business, or he asks whether he can pencil in the date for the client. This happens for only one reason, which we might just as well face; the salesman funks asking for the business. There is an old story in selling circles about the man who makes a perfect presentation to a client and nothing happens. So he adds still more Customer Benefits (reasons for buying), makes the proposition still more attractive and still nothing happens. Eventually out of sheer desperation he blurts out at the client, 'Well, why don't you buy it?' and the client yells back, 'Because you haven't asked me to!'

How do you ask? In two parts. First you check that the time is ripe. So we say.

'Is there any other information I can give you, Mr Coxwell?'

'No, I don't think so.'

We check again. 'Are there any problems which we have failed to resolve?' Notice 'we have failed'. This is a partnership; you're sitting on his side of the desk to make the event a great success, remember?

'No, I can't see any problems.'

Now having checked, you ask for the business. 'Can I book the date for you definitely then ?'

And, because I love stories with happy endings, Mr·Coxwell says, 'Yes, all right.'

Follow-ups

Now that Mr Coxwell has given us the business, can we relax and talk about the chances of Queens Park Rangers doing the double, or how to keep the lawn free of weeds? No, we certainly cannot. We now have an excellent opportunity to carry out some valuable market research, and we also have one or two loose ends to tie up. You will remember that we haven't found out yet whether the party at the Chairman's house in the Spring produces a need for overnight accommodation. And we haven't discussed the accommodation that may be wanted for this dinner. We know very little of the total demands of Canwe, Seldom and Co for hotels throughout the year and nothing at all about Mr Coxwell's private needs: is he the Chairman of the Golf Club; does he organise his Boy Scouts reunion; a Masonic Ladies' night or a dozen other events? No, we have a great deal of work to do yet. The amount of profit which is wasted by salesmen who turn off as soon as they have got the piece of business under discussion is a major criticism of their performance. Where do we start again? With the accommodation.

'Do you make arrangements for the accommodation of your guests, Mr Coxwell, or do they do it individually?' The last thing you want is for them to do it individually, because you can hardly ring all 150 of them. The question is designed to identify what is happening at the moment, not what you intend to happen in the future.

'They make their own arrangements. I tell them where we're holding the dinner and let them get on with it.'

This is sensible because it gives Mr Coxwell the minimum of work, it gives the executives the maximum of freedom, and there's the least paperwork for the company because the guests pay their bills on departure and recover the money through the petty cash. Perfectly reasonable, but no good to us. How to change the policy is the only problem.

'The trouble with everybody staying together, Mr Coxwell, is that it gives you a fair amount of work organising rooming lists and things like that.' You have to be a little vague. The company's procedures are not known to you, and the important thing is to let the client know that you recognise administrative problems too.

'Yes, it would be a nuisance for that reason.' We phrased the question so that Mr Coxwell is still saying 'yes'.

'We do have a method of overcoming the problem, because there are three advantages to getting everybody together. First, there is a further opportunity late in the evening and at breakfast for mixing together. The *esprit de corps* is given more time to flourish. Second, you know that everybody is safe – no driving after the dinner. And 35 per cent of fatal accidents do happen when a

63

driver has had a drink or two.' We don't have to announce that we think some of Mr Coxwell's guests are going to be stoned out of their minds by the end of the evening, but the message still arrives in a rather more delicate manner. 'Third, if the company books all the accommodation, I am sure we can offer you a wholesale rate for the booking so that you'd be likely to save money' (1).

'Did you say that you had a way round the paper work?' asks Mr Coxwell.

'Yes, we can provide you with a number of prepaid reply cards. You send these to the executives attending the dinner with the information that the company has made a block booking and ask them to communicate with the hotel direct. No paper work for you, but the company saves money and the benefit of the evening continues after the dinner is over.'

'It certainly makes sense,' says Mr Coxwell. 'What sort of price could you offer us?'

So we name a price. 'How would that compare with the allowance the company gives its senior executives?'

It might take a little haggling, but if we want the business because it fills beds that would otherwise be empty, we will reach a satisfactory compromise with Mr Coxwell in time. The important thing was to get over the problem of changing the present company procedure. Once he had agreed to that, the rest is simple.

We now want to do the market research on other business. If we simply ask whether Mr Coxwell knows anybody else who needs us, the benefit appears to be exclusively ours. There is nothing in it for him. The subject has to be introduced more subtly, then.

'How are you finding business this year, Mr Coxwell?'

We listen attentively. It doesn't matter whether the answer is good or bad, though if we can suggest some new method or new client, this is the opportunity to pay Mr Coxwell back for a substantial piece of business. The fact that you sold, rather than the client bought, still leaves you firmly in his debt. When the client has finished, the market research can be logically introduced, thus:

'Of course, the basic problem in industry in holding unit costs down is to achieve the highest turnover. We have this problem to an acute extent in the hotel industry because our product has no shelf life.'

Most businessmen have never thought of hotels as an industry. The use of 'unit costs' as a description of the sale of a bedroom, the marrying of a bedroom with a tin of beans in terms of 'shelf life' makes you a professional businessman in front of the client, rather than an amateur. 'Shelf life' is, of course, the technical term for how long a product can be on a supermarket shelf before it goes bad and cannot be sold. As a hotel bedroom has to be sold on the day it is prepared or perish for ever, we can say that our product has no shelf life at all.

'Yes, that must make life very difficult.'

'So the best way we can keep our prices down to all our customers is to try to achieve the maximum occupancy possible.'

'You ought to talk to Jerry Floyd,' says Mr Coxwell. 'He's in charge of our training department, and I know he uses hotels a lot.'

Sometimes you don't even have to ask. The client offers you the help you need. On other occasions you may specifically ask for the information. The important thing is that you have given Mr Coxwell a customer benefit. There is more likelihood that he will pay less in future if you are successful in keeping up your occupancy when he doesn't need you. That is, of course, perfectly true, as all customer benefits should be.

We continue the market research, not forgetting the social functions organisers. We finish up with four other executives of Canwe, Seldom & Co who use hotels a lot, one annual school dinner organiser, and a friend who organises conferences for a trade union. An impressive haul, but then there are few people who do not know somebody who organises an event at a hotel.

We are coming to the end of our meeting. Mr Coxwell has nearly finished his coffee, he has accepted a small brandy and a Petit Corona Havana. We haven't forgotten to offer him the best the restaurant can provide, because there is no point in spoiling the ship for a hap'orth of tar.

'We're very grateful, Mr Coxwell. Now is there anything else I can do for you?' This is not an invitation to accept a fiver under the table. Over the years I have done hundreds of small jobs which the clients considered favours but which were really very little trouble at all. The Trade Union official who had never been able to trace the biography of the founder of his union; we got that through the library system for him. Another wanted a run-down on the best hotel in some obscure Spanish island where he was taking a holiday; one of our Spanish travel agent friends provided that information. A third rang many years ago and asked me to book him a table at a notorious rip-off night club, and to get them to accept his cheque. On that occasion I warned the client that he was heading for a dreadful dive but he insisted, so I booked the table and he was able to pay by cheque. The morning after his visit I was embarrassed to receive a £5 note in the post, and realised for the first time that hall porters are not necessarily underpaid! A lot of the clients ask hoteliers for advice, if given the opportunity, and if you can provide that extra little help, it means that you are just as interested in giving service as in taking their money. Which is the truth, because if you don't do the former, you don't get to do the latter.'

'Just see that it's a good evening. Remember it really is very important to us.'

'Mr Coxwell,' we can say with complete sincerity, 'If the evening is a success, you will want to come back to the hotel, so it is just as much in our interests to ensure that it is a good evening as it is in yours.' Which is absolutely true.

Promotional Material

4

Some people, when they are particularly annoyed, might use the phrase, 'I could tear him apart with my bare hands'. But it isn't, in fact, at all likely that they could do a great deal of damage with just their bare hands. It would certainly be much quicker and more effective to use a blunt or pointed instrument in addition. The same is true of selling banquets, that most people prefer to ignore the help of good promotional aids and rely instead on their bare hands. Whether this is laziness, lack of foresight or misplaced economy, it is still a mistake.

There are a number of promotional aids which any hotel can possess, and we will examine these in some detail. Specifically there are specimen menus, banquet wine lists, photographs of the facilities, floor plans and publicity material.

Specimen Menus

The most common promotional aid is, of course, the specimen menu, and it is also probably the most important. Now what is a specimen menu? It is effectively the brochure for your product. If you went into a shop to buy a refrigerator, the proprietor would show you the appliance and give you a brochure produced by the manufacturer which would provide you with all the details of the product. When a client is going to buy a function, we show him the room and give him a specimen menu. So that the piece of paper, the sample menu, is a brochure for an expenditure of – what? Say 50 people at £3 a head, i.e. £150; or 200 people at £4 a head, i.e. £800; and if they buy the menu, they are obviously going to drink, so that the menu itself is only part of the expenditure. Now does your piece of paper look worth several hundred pounds – or over £1,000? Does it look worth 27½p?

Most sample menus do not. They look like rubbish and, to make matters worse, many hotels save paper by printing more than one menu on a sheet! They are trying to sell hundreds of pounds' worth of goods and they are intent at the same time on saving sheets of paper! Not even the thick, glossy art paper the cooker manufacturers use in full colour for their products, but our thin letterheads. That is if specimen menus are allowed to be printed on letterheads at all; there are any number of hotels who even save letterheads, and print the sample menus on plain paper! To make matters even worse – if that were possible – the menus, themselves, are often smudgily produced and inaccurately spelt.

At the very least, specimen menus should be printed on letterheadings, and there should be only one to a page. If they can be professionally printed, so much the better, but if they are to be typed, then the typing must be impeccable. This means that dishes in French should have the appropriate accents. If your typewriter does not have any accents, ask your local supplier to get you two new keys, and replace the ⅛/⅜ and ⅝/⅞ keys with the accents. You get grave and acute, circumflex and cedilla instead. You use accent keys by typing the accent before the letter. When you type the accent, the typewriter does not move forward so that the letter can still be typed in the appropriate space.

It also means that there must be no spelling errors, and that if anything needs to be erased by the secretary, it must be done perfectly. Clumsy half-erasures look grubby and, if your menu presentation is grubby, don't be surprised if the client wonders whether the food is going to be equally unappetising. The fact that the two pieces of work are done by two totally different people and that one has no relevance to the other, is unimportant in the eyes of the client. As far as he is concerned, the specimen menus and the banquet itself are products of the hotel as a whole, and everybody will be judged by the same yardstick. And he does want some yardstick by which to judge. He appreciates that everybody is going to *tell* him that things will be perfect, but he wants more than that. He wants to judge in advance by what he sees, and one of those judgements can be made on the basis of the sample menu presentation.

Typing menus perfectly is one thing. Reproducing them in bulk perfectly is something else again. There are many excellent means of reproducing material but any machine is only as good as its operator. It is the standard you want to set that determines the appearance of the result. Crumpled paper, duplicating the menus askew instead of absolutely straight, ink specks on the plate, a faded impression by not using enough ink or a worn-out typewriter ribbon, and poor layout are just some of the common errors in specimen menu presentation. Avoid them all by deciding upon a standard which will as closely as humanly possible reproduce the appearance of a piece of work by a professional printer.

If we go back to the brochure for the refrigerator for a moment. I wonder how many appliances would be sold if the brochure had no pictures and was printed entirely in Japanese? Effectively, we used to do something very similar. In years gone by, when all menus were in French without explanations, we did send out wording which many of the customers could not understand. Only once did a client ask me what I was trying to get him to buy with my *Selle d'Agneau*. After that I always put explanations under any dish which was not absolutely clear. What client wants to look an idiot by admitting that he isn't as clever as you when it comes to deciphering menus? Do you like to tell people that you are ignorant on a subject? Neither does the customer. Today it is much more generally accepted that menu dishes should be explained, but we very seldom use photographs of the dishes. It used to be difficult to photograph food and reproduce the prints well and cheaply, but these difficulties have now been overcome. What remains a problem is whether you can place on the banquet guest's plate a fair copy of the photograph you showed the organiser. The vast majority of hotels consider that they cannot, but they are certainly missing a fine promotional aid. One of the great advantages of a photograph is that it cuts out the necessity to build up a picture from the words which otherwise must describe the dish. A photograph of *Sole Bonne Femme* looks eminently more convincing than a description of 'Fillets of Sole in a mushroom, cream and white wine sauce, surrounded by a piping of Duchesse Potato'.

As you can see from the illustration overleaf, a photograph really does look worth the money the menu will cost the customer, but such a process may be too expensive for many hotels who will have to continue to rely on the written menu.

There is a still better method than the sample menu, and that is the full list of banqueting dishes you are able to offer. To proffer a list complete with prices has many advantages over the simple specimen menu. To begin with, it ensures that you are not offering the client a dish he does not like. I was once speaking to a lady in Newcastle, the mother of the bride, who assured me that she was not using a competitor's hotel because she didn't like *Pâté Maison*. The sample menu she had received included *Pâté Maison* and she did not realise that this – or any other item – could be altered. She had assumed that everybody who celebrated their marriage at the hotel had to have *Pâté Maison*. She didn't want it, so she wasn't going there. I would hope that most people know that this isn't the case, but we do tend to overestimate the knowledge of our customers. Even if the client knows he can change the menu, he is not always aware of the cost of doing so. The sample menu may specify soup, and they want *Pâté Maison* instead. By how much, they ask themselves, will the cost of the menu rise? Without contacting the hotel again, they cannot find out. With a list of banqueting dishes they can.

The long list also involves what salesmen call the principle of minimum

An example of a visual sample menu, normally supplied as a colour print.

choice. A client starts off with the idea that maybe he will use your hotel or maybe he will use someone else's; that is maximum choice. If he gets involved in the selection of menus with your list, he subtly – and to some extent subconsciously – moves to a decision on whether to have x or y for the main course. Whatever decision he reaches now, he has already made up his mind to use your hotel; that is the minimum choice, and obviously it is a position you want to reach. Another advantage of the long list is that it avoids the client saying 'No'. As we have seen, every time the client mentally says, 'Yes, I like that', you move one step nearer your goal of obtaining the booking. A sample menu where he says, 'Brussels sprouts! I can't stand Brussels sprouts,' is a 'no' position, and these are avoided by professional salesmen like the plague.

Indeed, I never do use sample menus when I am selling a banquet, for all those reasons and a few more. For instance, the alternative to the dish you dislike is the one you enjoy. I would therefore endeavour to discuss menus in terms of the client's own preferences. I would explain that it was quite impossible to design a menu which everyone would like when 50 or 150 people sat down for a meal, and consequently the sensible thing to do was to agree a menu of all the dishes the client himself liked. After all, I would say, the client was going to do all the work, so why shouldn't he at least enjoy his dinner. By the time we had finished agreeing a menu composed exclusively of dishes the client loved, I was that much ahead of the competition. Even if they had provided a sample menu of dishes which the client didn't actively dislike, there was no way in which they could have stumbled across a combination of everything he most enjoyed. When a client is comparing venues, his own tastebuds should always be working for you!

Another advantage of the long list is that the client often selects a menu above the price he originally had in mind. To get banqueting business, too many hotels have a tendency to start right at the bottom of the price list. If menus start at £3, then the one which is shown first isn't over £3. With a list, you can mention a minimum price but the client, by selecting his own dishes, may well finish up paying considerably more. It is like those numerous trays of sweets in a chain store. You intend to restrict yourself to a quarter of a pound, but by the time you've had a few of these and a few of those, you finish up with at least double that.

When it comes to describing the dishes, the hotel industry is still not far away from the days when no explanation was given at all; so it is not surprising that the terms used are still pretty basic. *Carré d'Agneau* might be explained as Best End of Lamb, but is it described as the most succulent, meatiest lamb chops? In America, mouth-watering descriptions are of ancient lineage. I can remember, twenty years ago, going to a Revue on Broadway where one sketch was entitled *And then I wrote . . . .* It was in the days when film biographies of song-writers were all the rage and, as a skit, it showed this character who wrote menu descriptions. Now somewhere between the hogwash of mushrooms 'hand picked at dawn in the dewy green meadows of enchanted Welsh valleys' and a description of *Sole Colbert avec Pommes Allumettes* as 'fish and chips', we have to find a policy for a terminology which helps to sell the dishes.

What rules can we lay down?

1. Be careful of words which worry the weight-conscious. Use words like 'rich', 'heavy' and 'thick' sparingly, because whilst there are still some people, like Billy Bunter of old, who seek out the calorie-filled items, there are far more who will be dreading getting on their scales the next morning.

2. An explanation should explain. I agree that this sounds pretty simple – unless you have seen on as many occasions as I have, *Omelette Surprise* described as a 'surprise omelette'.

3. Don't overestimate the intelligence of the customers. You know what *Poire Belle Hélène* is, I know what *Poire Belle Hélène* is, but it is a mistake to assume that all the customers do as well.

4. There are some very good words which deserve much more exposure, like 'fresh', 'tender', 'fluffy', 'soft', 'piping hot', 'juicy', 'home-made' and 'garnished'. The impression given is of newness and lightness, things which are not mass-produced but prepared with personal care. Obviously no list I could give would cover every possible dish, but within these criteria, you can build your own attractive language of explanations.

The dishes will be priced, and when inflation is upon us, the argument is sometimes made that it is difficult to forecast prices months ahead. This is true, but it is equally possible that some strike, meteorological hiccup, or unexpected shortage can affect prices at only a few weeks' notice. Accurate forecasting may be impossible, but the client is not concerned with this. Part of his decision-making process on using an hotel is usually based on whether he is satisfied with the contents of the menu he is promised. Of course, if you can get the business without dealing with the question of the menu until much nearer the date of the function, so much the better. If you cannot, it is better to lose a little of the profit on the menu, because of unexpected price increases, than lose the whole function through not being prepared to use the menu discussion as part of the selling process.

The classic way of presenting menus is to centre them up, as in Fig. 2, opposite, but to line up the menus from the left looks much more modern. We will ignore the fact that this way is also much less time-consuming, because producing it correctly matters far more than doing it quickly; but in any case, the centred-up menu is now passé. When one-off menus are produced on the centred-up basis, the centring is often wrong and looks it. A presentation like Fig. 3, overleaf, is neater, fresher and up-to-date.

The King William Hotel
Cathedral Square, Barchester S4U 3WS
Telephone: (0998) 121 5661 Telex: 123456 Cables: DOMESDAY

CANWE, SELDOM & CO. LTD.
CHAIRMAN'S DINNER

French Onion Soup

Fresh Trout with
Almonds

Caneton Montmorency
(with black cherries)
Pommes Sautées
Petits Pois au Beurre

Popacatapetl
(chestnut purée and
meringue)

Coffee

* * * *

Maçon Blanc 1973
La Cour Pavillon 1971

Liqueurs

Banquet Wine Lists

Banquet wine lists are invariably smaller and less impressive than the main wine list. Obviously they have a smaller selection because an hotel cannot stock very large quantities of more than a few wines. The days when hotels, such as the Metropole in Brighton, had room for 180,000 bottles in the cellars have long since gone. Even 1,000 would be considered a large stock today for all but the biggest hotels. The fact that the banquet wine list has to be restricted does not mean that it need appear to be. The answer is to pad it out with descriptions, illustrations, borders, potted histories and whatever else will cover up its limitations.

A lot of this information will be helpful anyway because, of course, the vast majority of the guests blindfold could not tell one wine from another. Nor, for that matter, could most management tell one claret from another, or distinguish between two hocks; but we won't tell the customers that because it would spoil our image!

Most wine lists in this country need to be re-examined with the thought in mind that this is 1979 and not 1879. The present documents are poor salesmen for us because they are based on the clientele of a bygone age. We would all agree that a wine list is a catalogue – a promotional piece produced exclusively to sell wine. For this purpose it normally includes the name of the wine, the vintage, the district, the shipper and the price. With that information, a Victorian connoisseur would be able to select exactly what he wanted. Today few guests know one shipper from another, the decent vintages have become very expensive indeed, we are drinking far more non-vintage wine, and some of the exotic titles which are being produced are extremely unlikely to get within loud-hailing distance of a 5me Cru. Indeed, the whole Cru system is pre-*Phylloxera*, as is well known, and therefore subject to distortion. Briefly the French classified their wines for quality before an insect attacked the vines in the late nineteenth century. When the vines recovered, the wines they produced were different, but they were never reclassified.

We are, in fact, dealing with a product where the purchasing is done on emotion more than anything else. As with cigarettes or beer, it is the beautiful blonde, the modern or traditional impression of the label, the snob appeal or the youthful attraction which sells the wine. There is nothing of this in the normal hotel wine list, because we seldom describe the wines in the first place; on those rare occasions when a hotel does so, it uses the sort of wording which is satirised in phrases like, 'I think you will be amused by its pretensions'. We talk about 'full-bodied' wines and 'light' wines as if those words really meant something.

Start again, therefore, and divide your wine list up so that it appeals to as

The King William Hotel
Cathedral Square, Barchester S4U 3WS
Telephone: (0998) 121 5661 Telex: 123456 Cables: DOMESDAY

```
CANWE, SELDOM & CO. LTD.
CHAIRMAN'S DINNER


French Onion Soup

Fresh Trout with Almonds

Caneton Montmorency
(with black cherries)
Pommes Sautées
Petits Pois au Beurre

Popacatapetl
(chestnut purée and
meringue)

Coffee

*  *  *  *

Maçon Blanc 1973
La Cour Pavillon 1971

Liqueurs
```

many markets as you have wines; you can have one for the wine snob, 'a little-known chateau, but connoisseurs will recognise its quality'; another for the young ladies who want to enjoy themselves 'French, fun and frothy'; one for the older generation, 'Deservedly popular for many years'; one for the Club members, 'A good quaffing wine'; one for the 'sock-it-to-me' lads, 'Better drunk sitting down'; and so on. I know that this approach offends the wine snobs in the trade, but the objective is to sell wine, and the public buy more if this approach is followed in all but our best hotels. The idea emerged from a marvellous comment on advertising by Jerry Della Femina, an author I thoroughly recommend. In his book I mentioned earlier, *From Those Wonderful Folk Who Gave You Pearl Harbour,* Mr Della Femina recalls that the most success-ful beer advertisement for many years was the one which said, 'The only one to have when you're having more than one'. The promise to heavy drinkers was apparently irresistible.

In my own wine list, I have described the carafe wines as 'We're proud of our Spanish plonk'. Apart from improving the credibility of the list ('If they call it plonk, the rest of the list must be honestly described as well'), it did result in the customers 'trading up'. Previously mothers of the bride, for example, had been satisfied with carafe wine, though they knew it was plonk. But now that the hotel jovially admitted it, they felt that it wasn't right for their daughter's wedding and bought more expensive wines. These, of course, are more profitable for the hotel.

Presentation Books

There is a speech in *Henry V* where Chorus asks his audience to imagine the battle of Agincourt because they can't get it on stage! 'Piece out our imperfec-tions with your thoughts' may be reasonable enough in the theatre, but it isn't very helpful when the client is trying to decide whether to use your banqueting room or not. Yet when he goes into the room for the first time, the overwhelm-ing likelihood is that it is not set up for his numbers or with the lay-out he would want. On many occasions the room will not be set up at all, but will – in the morning, for example – still bear the scars of the night before. The client will appreciate that it has to be cleared of the debris of the previous evening, but how can he judge a room when stained tablecloths, full ash-trays, stacked chairs and unwashed glasses litter the scene? When it really matters, you can specifically offer to set up the room for the client exactly as it would be for his own function, so that when he arrives he sees it in perfect condition. But this is obviously not feasible with every customer and, even if it is immaculately set up for a dinner, if he wants to use the room for a conference, there will still be the problem of visualising the setting.

The answer, of course, is to have a presentation book of photographs so that the customer can see his approximate arrangement whatever the state of the room. As we all know, a colour photograph taken by a competent photographer can often look better than the actual product. Then the customer does not have to imagine; he can see for himself. In my view, presentation books – which should also include other material we will discuss in a moment – are worth their weight in gold, yet few hotels use them. They do, admittedly, take a lot of putting together and cost a fair amount of money. But see what benefits they can bring you.

In 1963, I knew that in a year's time we were going to have a new banqueting room at the Europa Hotel, capable of seating 500 guests, and in competition with the best hotels in Mayfair. As the hotel was still in the process of being built, any customer who wanted to see the setting was, at best, going to have to navigate the builder's scaffolding, materials and ladders in order to reach a concrete cavern which looked about half as attractive as a long disused aircraft hanger. The only solution was to show the room by means of an artist's impression and floor plans. Over the course of that next twelve months we sold nearly £200,000 worth of banqueting – and remember those are 1964 pounds, where a good four-course dinner was only about £3 a head. At the time of writing – fifteen years later – we still look after a tailoring federation I sold to successfully at that time. I well recall lugging the presentation book to Covent Garden to show it to the committee across a desk like a billiard table. They bought this unbuilt hotel against stiff competition from a top restaurant and a top, old-established Mayfair hotel.

The presentation book must have more than photographs. It must also have floor plans; these can be drawn by hand, so long as they are neat. The plans enable you to show the client exactly where each table will go, why you can't get more than 75 people on a top table, where the microphone points are to be found, and how large is the dance floor. Show the room set in as many ways as you like – round tables, top and sprigs, herring-bone, classroom fashion, cinema style and so on. Set it up for maximum numbers with every table in, and show how the layout can be just as effective with half that number by leaving more space, putting in more serving tables and so on.

My presentation book in 1963 had some other qualities as well. How could I impress the clients with the style of the hotel when they couldn't even see it except as a building site? The same applies to your hotel, because although you can show the room set up, you can't show the style of service or the standards you provide. When all you have is a building site, it concentrates the mind splendidly. My wife advised me that what I needed to convey elegance and style was a chocolate-coloured cover with the hotel's name picked out in gold lettering, and coffee-coloured pages. She was absolutely right, even though I had to scour London to find a supplier of chocolate-coloured covers and coffee-coloured pages. Black covers and plastic holders for the pictures may be practical and effective, but they are neither elegant nor stylish.

Another problem we had at the Europa was how to persuade anybody that we could cook. The hotel wasn't even open, so how could we guarantee the standard of the cuisine? And how can you guarantee yours? The answer, we decided, was to include in the presentation book sample menus of two kinds. One was a set of national menus, offering complete French, German, Dutch, Italian and many other specifically national meals. This gave the impression that the hotel was prepared and able to cook any type of food. Far from playing it safe, the hotel was offering the widest selection of dishes. We also took some of the menus which had been prepared by Escoffier for important events, like the visits to Britain of the Kaiser or the French Prime Minister at the turn of the century, and simply priced them for 1964. We described what the menus were and offered to serve them; the implication was that anything Escoffier could do, we could do just as well. Those menus were in the book solely to prove the quality of an untried cuisine, and they played their part in achieving that objective. The fact that none of the menus was actually bought by a client, even once, was quite unimportant.

In your presentation book there should be examples of menus you have served for important functions in your hotel. If you are good enough for those events, you should be good enough for the new client. Associated with this idea, there should be photographs in your office of you greeting important guests. The fact that you deal with these V.I.P.s and yet are anxious to look after the client who is possibly not so famous, is an excellent piece of goodwill building. The famous never object to being photographed with you because they often stay famous only because of all the publicity they get!

So in your presentation book you will have photographs, floor plans, special menus, menus of important functions you have done, and, of course, the banqueting wine list.

The book should also double as a scrapbook for you. It should include press cuttings of past events (favourable ones!) and any photographs you took at the time of particularly well-produced buffets, displays, imaginative banquet dishes and special menus. It is like the paraphenalia you see around you in an old theatre; you get a sense of greatness just by being there, because so many great people have been there before you, so many important events have taken place where you are standing. The same impression should be given of your hotel.

As you look at the pristine splendour of your presentation material, spare a thought for the way it is going to look when it arrives in the post on the client's desk. All too often it gets there crumpled and dog-eared, because you haven't taken sufficient care to put the material into stout enough packaging. What precautions can you take?

1. Always put the material into an envelope large enough to hold it without folding, if it wasn't designed to be folded. A letter obviously is designed to be folded, and a brochure isn't.
2. See that the envelope you use has cardboard backing, like the envelopes used by photographers to send prints through the post.
3. Send one sample of the material you will be sending out regularly to yourself first. Just put all you normally send to a client into an envelope and post it to yourself. Look at its condition when it arrives and you will know what the client will be seeing.
4. Remember that other people are handling your precious presentation material. Secretaries can fold letters clumsily, so that the folds are not clean cut. Post rooms can bundle the material up with string, cutting into the sides. It may help the Post Office but it doesn't do your presentation any good at all. There is no harm in having printed on the envelope 'Photographs. Handle with care'.

It is not just the material you send out which should reflect well on you. It is also the material you use on the night of the function. The appearance of the table plan, the seating plan, the place cards and the menu are important because they help to give a good impression. Who knows why any individual client chooses to return to the same hotel? If every small detail is handled correctly, you must improve your chances. The seating plan is a problem because only the shape of the room can be printed, and the actual table placing has to be drawn. It is a time-consuming and very difficult job if the finished plan is not to appear the work of an amateur. If possible, the seating plan should be used only as a working drawing for the committee to organise who sits where. If it has to be on display in the banqueting room, then you just have to go to the necessary effort to make it look professional. Draw carefully and tidily. Put the table plan on to a large sheet of very good paper with the hotel heading at the top.

There are a number of opportunities to promote a hotel by name which are often missed. This is one of them, and another is the lectern from which the speaker delivers his address. Very often these are not labelled at the front with the name of the hotel, but since the audience is – hopefully – looking at the speaker most of the time, this chance to implant the name of the hotel in their minds should not be wasted.

The typed seating plan should also be on the headed paper of the hotel, and again it should be paper of a higher than normal quality. The cost involved is negligible in terms of the bill for a function, but so often management will not spend the money because they feel it is wasted. Not so; it is the little things which reflect the thought and care a hotel puts into the detailed planning of functions. Even with an item as small as the place card, there is no reason why it should be completely plain. Each card should carry the name of the hotel or the name of the major suite if that is a selling point for you. It can be produced with a cut-out so that the name (Fig. 4) stands out to an even greater extent. Don't forget that many customers are using your hotel specifically to impress their guests with the quality of their hospitality. The clients want to boast a little by bringing to the attention of the guests that they are in your hotel rather than one that is less attractive. If, therefore, the name of your hotel is more prominent, it will not irritate the clients.

In some cases the client wants to have the menu printed himself, in which case its final appearance is not within your control. That should not prevent you from discussing the matter with the client, because if you are planning to use the pink tablecloths, and he comes up with an orange menu cover, the two are going to clash horribly. Anything looks good on a white tablecloth, but if there are different colours being used, try to ensure that the end result is harmonious.

If you are producing the menus yourself in the hotel on a duplicating machine, have a double card so that it stands by itself, rather than a single card which has to rest against something. Print the hotel's name on the cover and use a good quality cartridge paper. Art-coated papers for menus look glossy but they also look cheap. The people who are going to look at the menus when at the table or when they get home are not necessarily your customers at the moment, but every one of them might be a potential customer. Ensure, therefore, that the printed material they see is part of your sales approach to them. We all hope to have letters which say, 'I was at a function in your hotel last week and was so impressed I would like to know if you can look after my dinner'. But what particularly impressed that guest? It could be anything, and therefore look at the presentation of everything with that in mind.

What do we feel about promotional give-aways: the pencils and ball-point pens with the hotel's name on them, the notebooks and pads of paper? Anything which stays on a businessman's desk for a long time is a good idea, because it keeps your name in front of him. Anything which is going to be given to the children, wear out or go wrong is not good. A lot of hotels provide these items as conference equipment, but I don't believe it brings one extra customer into the hotel. The items are not an intrinsic part of the function and therefore their absence does not affect anything.

Remember that the most dangerous problem you face with promotional material is your own laziness; that you can't be bothered to get all the 'bumf' together before you see the client, can't be bothered to lug it around and get it in

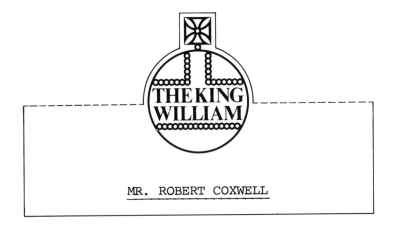

MR. ROBERT COXWELL

Figure 4. A cut-out place card using the King William logo.

the right order and check the details. It *is* a nuisance, but the correct selling of banquets requires that these small points are carried out correctly. A polished presentation should not leave the client to imagine anything, if it is possible to show it to him instead.

One last point about promotional material. Do not make the mistake of asking the client to read a document and then talk while he is doing so. People cannot read and listen at the same time. Try doing that yourself and you will find it is true; you can't read a book and concentrate on a news broadcast; you do one or the other. The customers can look and listen, but even as they look, you should pause in your presentation. This gives the client the opportunity to think about what he is seeing; again, you cannot think about one thing and listen attentively to another. If the client looks at a photograph of a dinner dance and thinks of the floral decorations which will be needed, he cannot at the same time absorb what you are saying about the air conditioning. Just because the client is less than a yard away from you does not automatically guarantee that he can hear what you are saying in a normal voice. Pauses are essential, with a test question like, 'Am I making sense?' or 'Does that sound reasonable?' This offers the client the opportunity to catch up, and on occasions to rejoin you from his reverie. Watch his eyes; they often give you a clue that he has wandered mentally out of earshot.

5

Creative Banqueting

Many functions are held with the purpose of getting some of the guests to remember a particular point; the salesmen to remember the details of a new product, the travel agent to remember the destinations to which the airline flies, the press to remember a company's name. It is possible to reinforce the message the client is trying to put over by introducing aspects of it into some of the areas for which the hotel is responsible – the menu, for example. Other functions are held in honour of an individual or a company; when someone retires, when an association meets for its New Year Ball, when an annual staff party is held. Then the organisation would like to get its image more firmly embedded in the minds of the guests, and this too can be emphasised in the arrangements the hotel makes.

The Victorians were masters of this type of creative banqueting. They named dishes after famous guests, produced a wide variety of consumable objects in sugar work and ice work, made marvellous effects with flambé cooking and generally showed great imagination. We have to learn these lessons again because they are still powerful weapons in getting the client to choose your hotel rather than another. But they are weapons which, for most hotels, are growing rusty. Admittedly there are a very few hotels which can get all the business they need, simply because they have the finest chefs, the most splendid décor, the most impeccable service and a clientele which can afford the enormous cost which such standards inevitably demand. I was never so fortunate in the product I had to sell, but happily this also meant that I was needed because the product didn't sell itself! My clients were not going to be wildly impressed with the décor of my hotels in the 1950s, they very often knew of better standards of service and cheaper prices. It was a question of 'be creative or die'. Most hotels today could rapidly increase their banqueting turnover if they accepted that the same stimulus still applies.

How to Sell Banquets

Let me give you one example, and then we will examine all the possible areas where imagination can help the client to achieve his objectives. Airlines are very generous with their hospitality, and at Christmas-time in particular, the travel agents are invited to a large number of parties. Many years ago I was asked to handle a cocktail party for an airline which did not even fly into London. They wanted the agents to memorise those cities to which they did fly, and to remember which airline had given the party. The prospects were not encouraging. If the airline handed out the route map as a brochure, the chances were that most of them would be thrown away outside the hotel as just another load of 'bumf'. If one of the officials made a speech telling the guests of the cities covered, the likelihood of their even paying attention, during a party, was remote. Posters could be put up around the walls, but everyone put up posters and they would hardly attract attention.

I suggested two contributions the hotel could make which would solve the problem. First, a three-foot-long cake with the map of the world piped on the icing. On the map of the world we would place plaques for each town to which the airline flew, and connect them up with the route map in a different coloured icing. Now the agents had not seen a three-foot-long cake as frequently as they had seen brochures! Indeed, most of them could never have seen a cake that long at all. Therefore, after being received by their host, they could be guided towards the cake. As there would be little else to do at the party, they could gaze at it admiringly for several seconds or even minutes, thereby absorbing the details of the route map. This they did, willingly!

The second suggestion was based on the fact that at the time the airline flew to sixteen different national cities. There were obviously going to be canapés served to the guests, but instead of the normal selection it was agreed that each tray would be labelled with the name of one of the appropriate cities, and consist of one of that city's specialities. So if the city was Honolulu, the canapés would be pineapple chunks with cheese; if it was Rome it would be slices of pizza. Each time a guest took a canapé, he was reminded of the name of one of the airline's destinations.

The hotel I suggested for the party was not brilliant. But the ideas were good, and the client bought the ideas. You might imagine that clients would listen to good ideas and then take them to a better hotel, but in my experience this very rarely happens. Almost invariably, if the client buys the ideas, he buys the hotel. Before we tackle the large subject of menus, let us take some of the peripheral aspects of banqueting first.

Flowers

As many companies, associations and teams have their own symbolic colours, it is a good idea, wherever possible, to feature these colours in the flower designs. If you can find fresh flowers in these colours, so much the better. If not, it is quite possible to spray fresh flowers – carnations in particular – in practically any shade you want. The result is tasteful and does not harm the flowers at all. It is also possible to create a company crest in fresh flowers, much as one sees a floral clock or coat-of-arms in a seaside resort. Features of this kind can be a great help in selling a function.

Napkins

You can effectively use napkins as a memento of an occasion by using silk-screen printing to reproduce a design on the linen. In this way, you can print the menu – this saves you the cost of printing menus on card – or the new product, the association crest, the name of the company, anything. The result is a very good take-home present, much more likely to be kept and remembered than a piece of paper or a photograph. The extra cost is not so great when you bear in mind the saving on printed menus and on laundry – for these napkins will be taken away.

Menu Theming

The possibility of linking the menu to the theme of a conference is often open to us if we are prepared to take advantage of it. Let me give you an example. Some years ago there was a national sales conference for a large biscuit company. As the chairman of the meeting was named Macdonald, the organisers decided to take advantage of the great popularity of the James Bond books to link them to the conference. During the entire conference, the Chairman was referred to as 'M', the code name of the head of the Secret Service in the books. The salesmen were given point-of-sale material for a new product which was referred to as the weapon to be used, and the James Bond theme music was played to introduce the speakers. There were many other links, but you get the idea. Then it was up to the hotel to produce a menu for lunch which carried on the theme. This is what was served: From Aylesbury With Love, Boeuf Smersh Strogonoff, Goldfinger Potatoes, Albert R. Broccoli, Bombe Surprise. 'From Aylesbury With Love' was a wild duck soup with sherry, and pasta shaped in '0's and '7's. Smersh, aficionados of James Bond will remember, was the international enemy secret service and the alliteration is there with Eastern European overtones. 'Goldfinger Potatoes' were croquettes, which have something of the appearance of gold fingers. Albert R. Broccoli referred to the producer of the films. The Bombe Surprise was a Christmas pudding with a large white string fuse attached to it. The menu was a great success and the organiser was very pleased.

It is often felt that special menus for an event of this nature must be very expensive for the hotel to produce, and are likely to break the rules on balance, colour and so on. Let us examine this particular menu from those points of view. A consommé is the cheapest starter you can offer; Beef Strogonoff is usually produced from the cheaper cuts of meat, no matter what the official recipe demands; the vegetables are not expensive; and nor is the Christmas pudding. Indeed, it would be difficult to select a menu concocted of cheaper ingredients. Now let us look at colour; you have a dark brown starter, a pinkish main course with a light brown potato and a green vegetable. A black dessert with a yellow sauce. No problem there with the colours. What about balance? you have a light starter, a reasonably substantial main course and a heavy dessert. The balance is right for men with reasonable appetites. And, of course, a special menu like that, created specifically for the conference, can be priced rather higher than the individual dishes if they were simply produced as a sample menu for a lunch. If you know the theme of the function, you have the opportunity to contribute to its effectiveness.

As you would expect, many of the basic creative ideas repeat themselves as we go through the various courses, but the concepts vary considerably in cost. It helps to be able to quote the client for each different type of gimmick so that he doesn't get overenthusiastic about an idea he cannot possibly afford. For example, it is perfectly possible with melon or pineapple boats to have flags made to attach to the cocktail stick masts. However, the cost is high, for these are one-off productions and must be hand produced rather than printed. If, of course, the client has his own in-house art department, it can be less expensive for him, and if he can persuade his advertising agency to do the work as a favour, it will cost him less again!

The organisation is likely to want one or more of the following to be publicised: the name of a new product, the name of the company, the name of a guest, the names of the bride and groom, the company or association logo, the company colours or the company emblem. The ideas which follow can often be adopted for more than one of these items. I have usually specified only one item, but the multi-purpose uses are easily recognised.

Flags: Any kind of flags can be placed on the table, not just national ones. You can use the flag of a company or association.
Condiments: Salt and pepper can be put in a manufacturer's container of any description, with holes made in the top of the tin. If, for example, the new product is a new range of soups, salt and pepper can be shaken from the soup tins on the table.
Bread rolls: These can be produced in the shape of any letter the client likes at

very little extra cost. On a table for ten, for example, you can spell out Midland Bank or Pilkington.

Soup: Pasta letters in the soup can spell out the initials of the company or association. The cheese straws with a consommé can be shaped in letters or patterns as well.

Salade Mikado: As already mentioned, this is an hors d'oeuvres made with edible chrysanthemum petals. It can be produced for any organisation connected with agriculture; and is also popular in the fashion world.

Pineapple or Melon Boats: Decorate a design on a flag fixed to a cocktail stick mast (see above).

Oeuf en gelée: You can initial any dish *en gelée* with mayonnaise piping on the top.

Boeuf en croute: The pastry case can be used for a design or wording. This applies to pies of any descriptions, as well.

Coulibiac: The pastry case here too can be used for a design or emblem.

Potatoes: Can be produced in a variety of designs and emblems.

Cakes: The surface of an iced cake can be used as a drawing board for any design.

Ice-cream: Not only can models be made out of ice-cream but the model can be in the company's colours.

Chestnut purée: Most products or emblems can be shaped out of chestnut purée.

Dry ice: Dry ice is carbon dioxide frozen solid. It dissolves in water giving off harmless smoke. It must not be touched with the bare hands, nor must anyone be allowed to eat it, because it can burn the skin. In creative banqueting it can be used for many purposes; put it into the hollow chimney of a model ice-cream house and add water to it just before it is brought into the room – the smoke rising from the house chimney is very effective. Put it into the funnel of a model ship and the same effect results. Using dry ice under a protective covering at the base of a fruit salad bowl, the fruit salad is then brought in smoking, but is in fact getting colder all the time.

Custards, jellies, cheesecakes: The surface of all these desserts can be used for a design or emblem, as can éclairs, meringues and biscuits.

Sugar work and ice work: The most attractive designs can be produced with this kind of culinary artistry.

Macaroons: Write a message in vegetable inks on the rice paper.

Petits fours: These can be produced in a variety of designs, colours and emblems.

The ideas mentioned above are, in no way, a comprehensive list, but simply indicates that a very wide range of dishes can be adapted to do more than look attractive and provide the necessary number of calories. Furthermore, the dishes discussed are linked to publicising an aspect of the client's event.

Banners and Notice Boards

The American fashion of displaying jumbo-size banners welcoming the Shriners, General Motors or the Lady Dentists is a type of flattery which is a little too much for the British taste. We have now started to say 'welcome' in a way we consider more dignified if less striking. The first to copy the Odeon type of sign was the Heathrow Hotel at London Airport, which put up a display board on the main road. Even that remains too extreme for most British hotels, though De Vere have taken to heading their display boards within their hotels with the wording, for instance, 'The de Montfort welcomes . . .' followed by the day's function list. This is certainly an improvement on the days when conference traffic was considered a second-class citizen compared with the individual traveller. I would have expected an honest hotel in those immediate post-war days to put on the notice board, 'The Splendide is prepared to put up with . . .'! The client likes to see his own name prominently displayed, and many of them would appreciate a banner across the lobby announcing something like 'Welcome to the Cladworthy Rotary Club Dinner Dance'. Would anybody else be so irritated that they would never darken your door again? You must decide that for yourself, but if the banner were professionally produced, a lot of hotels would be improving their repeat business. Just as a client in the banqueting office may be impressed by photographs of the banqueting manager with important guests, so the clientele in the hotel may be equally impressed when they have the identity of other guests brought to their attention in such a way. After all, many ordinary guests may also be potential banqueting customers, and they might have been unaware of the quality or size of your banqueting facilities.

Notice boards are a marvellous way to upset customers! All you have to do is misspell their names. Time and again I have seen this done, and the reason is simple; the porters make up the banqueting board on the basis of the list sent to them by the banqueting department, and that list is usually typed by a secretary. If she types the name wrongly, then the porters will not correct it – or even know that it is wrong. It is therefore essential that the banqueting manager checks the list with particular care. The mistakes usually occur where an organisation or individual spell their name slightly differently from the norm, or when there are two ways of spelling a name. Davies and Davis, Phillip and Philip, Hyde and Hide. It happens less often with names like Brzynsky because the complicated nature of the spelling forces the secretary to concentrate. Always check initials as well. The organiser of the retirement dinner is not going to be pleased to see R. P. Fenton when it should be P. R. Fentone.

Most notice boards nowadays are of the kind where the letters are produced from an alphabet box and spelt out. This leads to another kind of error where the porters use discoloured or broken letters rather than search for better ones. To their eyes the result might be perfectly satisfactory, but it will not be to the client. If the 'L' is missing, the porter might use a capital 'I', a mistake which secretaries are prone to make when typing. Pick up these tiny points because they all help you towards a perfect job. There are enough mistakes to be made by accident without ignoring these areas where you know mistakes are likely.

How can you be creative with a notice board? The symbol of the organisation can be produced to go alongside the lettering, the lettering can be specially produced in the company's house colours or even in their logo. It is a small touch but it adds some additional personality to an area which is usually completely sterile, and therefore has greater impact.

There are also a large number of ways of creating a new atmosphere for a function. A client who has used a hotel for a year or two may feel that the excitement of the new venue is now wearing thin. All too often at this point he thinks in terms of changing to another hotel. He can easily be persuaded not to do so if you come up with new ideas for his evening. This is where the Country and Western evening, the Italian or Hawaiian evening, the 1920s or Victorian evening come into their own. With the use of costume for the staff, the appropriate type of cabaret and some audience participation, the event can be entirely different from year to year. The dishes comprising the menu are, of course, appropriate for the era or the nationality. These special evenings are a boon if you have an indifferent banqueting room, one where the quality of the décor does not really compare with a competing hotel. If you look at a stage on the morning after the performance, it doesn't look very glamorous, either, but at night when the lighting, the costumes and the music are all playing their part, it is transformed. So it can be with a hotel ballroom.

Remember that the client will get the credit for these ideas, but he will be expected to do better each year. To achieve that target he needs your expertise, and this is a powerful reason for coming back to you.

6

Sales Training

Your own ability to sell is one thing. Getting a sales team about you is another matter, but there is no way in which you can do all the selling yourself. The higher you are promoted and the bigger your company becomes, the less time you will have personally to sell, and the less impact your own efforts will make on the total clientele. In such an eventuality the greatest contribution you can make to turnover will be your degree of success in passing on your knowledge.

In this chapter we are going to look at the training problems which must be overcome.

To get more banquets, what personnel do we need to sell effectively? Not just the specialist salesmen; the telephonist, secretary, porters and receptionists all play their part as well. The banqueting department and any assistant management involved in banqueting do so too. Training them is not something that can be done *en bloc*, in a hurry or in a superficial way. It has to be carefully planned and carefully executed.

The first difficulty to be surmounted is the fact that many people do not *want* to sell. A busy telephonist finds it easier to be abrupt than courteous, a receptionist who has had trouble with her boy friend may prefer to take out her irritation on a client rather than be pleasant. One assistant manager may be terrified of selling anything to a client, and another may consider it beneath his dignity. One may be shy and another may be gauche. An old hand may have been taught that the client is fair game, and a young newcomer may not know his product at all well. You might be faced with every kind of difficulty, but there is always a solution if you tackle the problems systematically.

If you have a banqueting department, recognise that their expertise is more likely to be in running banquets than selling them. The traditional banqueting manager worked appalling hours, could manage extra ducks, knew how to serve the most complicated dishes, and how to put on a function with all the precision of the Changing of the Guard. He was not noted for his command of the English language or his sales ability; indeed he had precious little time for selling when he was organising and supervising the functions. He also had even less time to teach the complexities of selling, and so his juniors inevitably suffered. Verbal training isn't sufficient anyway, it is very important in all training to not only *say* what you want done, but to see that your instructions are available in writing. It is also vital to persuade people that your views are correct, rather than give orders; otherwise when your back is turned, the orders may not be carried out as you wish. You need to win over a man's mind rather than to dictate to him. I remember my old friend Brian Lees, the Managing Director of Playtex, who had a notice on the wall facing his desk which read, 'What you supervise gets done'. You must keep on checking that the work is being carried out properly.

The very beginning of the banqueting manager's job is to take the bookings that are offered, and that means having a banqueting book that everybody can read and keep up accurately. We have covered that in Chapter 2.

Next, we must overcome the blinkers that most banqueting managers have about booking hotel accommodation. They concentrate on the function and do not bother to sell the bedrooms because that is supposed to be solely the Reception Manager's job. As few Reception Departments are equipped with a crystal ball, how they are supposed to divine what enquiries have been made direct to the Banqueting Department is not explained. Obviously this can cost a fortune, because the profit on the bedrooms can be greater than the profit on the function. So all Banquet Detail Sheets should have a line for Accommodation just as there is a line for Menu or Wines. And put it in bold letters! It is indeed a vital part of sales training to get the reception department and the banqueting department working closely together. Not only can the banqueting people sell accommodation, but the receptionists can find clues to additional banqueting. For example, if you are running a city hotel and you get a reservation for a senior manager and his wife on a weekday, there is a strong likelihood that they are coming to a function in your town. That function could be held at your hotel next year if you take the trouble to identify it. But Reception usually miss the clues, and the reason is that they can't be bothered. They see no benefit from inspecting the correspondence carefully, and they feel they are working hard enough without taking on this additional chore. The banqueting department often have a number of deep-rooted objections to Reception and it is no use ignoring the fact. The banqueting department is often managed by an ex-waiter who might consider himself in the same category as a blue-collar worker. The receptionists are white-collar workers, and that is one barrier. Then the Reception Manager works much shorter hours than the Banqueting Manager, and this is resented. He has often had a better education too, which can create another barrier. He is also often younger but, even so, is more accepted as a member of the management team. Where the banquet department are heavily dependent on tips, the work they need to carry out to get bedroom bookings would be considered unproductive. So you see how it can happen that neither side wants to work with the other. It is the General Manager's job to see that they do. To achieve this the two departments should be brought together for training in the sales area. One good way is to manufacture two sets of identical correspondence, full of clues to more business. Then divide the departments into two mixed teams and offer a prize for the team that gets the most clues right. As they work together to beat the other team, you start to get a little more rapport. Keep pushing them together, make the respective managers lunch together with you, send them off occasionally to a catering exhibition or on a sales call together, have them home for dinner with their wives, and keep trying to make them into a team instead of two separate departments.

In teaching the banqueting management to sell, the first thing you have to do is decide where the time is coming from. Not just the time to learn sales techniques but also the time to practise them. Is the Banqueting Manager supposed to be a production manager, supervising the production line; or is that the job of the Head Waiter, leaving the Banqueting Manager time to sell? This is a problem you must resolve. It is useless during the height of the banquet season to say that the Manager can do both. If, for instance, the client says that he can come to lunch on Wednesday to discuss his major function, the Banqueting Manager can't refuse to see him on the grounds that he has to supervise a large lunch on that same day. Something has to give, and the best answer is to have more than one executive capable of supervising, and more than one capable of selling. It is a nonsense in the largest hotels that the Assistant Managers are seldom encouraged to sell banquet customers on the grounds that this would be seen as treading on the banquet department's toes. As a result the client is often not entertained at all, and when the Assistant Manager gets his own hotel, he has had little or no experience of selling and entertaining.

The Banqueting Manager may, at first, resent the help of the Assistant Managers on the often unspoken grounds that they are interfering, or reducing the Banqueting Manager's authority; the 'Stay out of my kitchen' syndrome. This complaint evaporates as soon as an Assistant brings home a piece of business by a successful interview. No Banqueting Manager in his right mind objects to competent help.

In training any young person to sell, the effort is greatest at the outset because all the difficult aspects of selling are in the young executive's mind;

the potential humiliation by imaginary unpleasant clients, the horrors of an examination where you don't know the answers, the ego-bruising overtones of 'touting for business' and so on. These feelings have to be understood. They are perfectly genuine, even if misguided. Some people do get nervous to the point of feeling sick, perspiring or getting headaches when they first try to sell. It is somewhat like making a speech in public for the first time; it is a bit nerve-racking. We all know that this sensation doesn't last; when a salesman has made a few sales presentations and as soon as he gets his first piece of business, he is over the hump for ever. There is a great deal of satisfaction in getting a client to accept your hotel, especially if he had doubts at the outset. When you persuade him that he need have no doubts and when he finally gives you the business, there is job satisfaction for you! That is the drug that keeps salesmen going and a very powerful one it is too. But top management have to provide the encouragement until success provides it for the young executive.

The effort needed to help the young salesman falls into two categories; explaining the technical details of the job and then making sure they are carried out. Without the supervision, the training might well be non-productive. One nervous young Assistant Manager was telling me that he found that selling over lunch ruined his digestion; it is a problem which is very common and the solution, I explained, was to eat very lightly indeed; the less you had to digest, the easier it would be for the stomach to do the job. 'No,' he said, 'I have found a much better solution than that.' I am always prepared to learn, so I asked him what was the secret. 'I eat just as much as I ever did,' he explained 'and I don't get indigestion, because we don't talk business!' A lot of people will pretend to do the selling job but will dodge the column on every possible occasion, simply because they need help in getting over those initial nervous hurdles.

Ideally, the process of teaching people to sell involves having them with you to watch you do it first, and then you watching them when they have absorbed a modicum of knowledge. The student should accompany you at sales presentations and he should carry a notebook. In that notebook he should put down every point about your presentation that he doesn't under-stand. 'Why did you use those particular words?', 'why did you introduce that topic of conversation?', 'why did you deal with that problem in that particular way?' Anything at all the student finds obscure should be written down and discussed with you afterwards. If he has nothing written down, the strong likelihood is that your pupil wasn't listening attentively. Apart from saying 'Good morning,' when the client arrives, the student is not there to contribute to the conversation; he is there to observe two other people talking. He should be warned right at the beginning to say nothing at all, because the inexperienced can usually – and naturally – be relied on to say the wrong thing. It is the old story of the motorist stopped by the policeman for speeding. Strenuously and convincingly he denies the charge until his wife says, 'Nonsense, dear, you must have easily been going 80 miles an hour.' The audience is not supposed to take part in the play.

When you feel that the younger executive is ready to start selling for himself, try to select a client who is not going to give him a difficult time, one who has used the hotel before and been well satisfied. If the young salesman can obtain the first piece of business he attempts, it is a great confidence booster.

I well remember my first appointment. It so happens that I started selling on a Tuesday, knowing nothing of selling or hotels. I made an appointment to see Peter Pratt, who was in charge of reservations for TWA. It was September, the most difficult month of the year for getting hotel space in London, although I didn't know it at the time. When I walked in to see Peter – my first client – he greeted me with, 'Boy, am I pleased to see you!' Many people weren't as friendly 25 years ago, and that was a tremendous boost.

As the young salesman makes his presentation, your greatest difficulty – as a trainer – is to keep quiet! Yes, we all know you could do it better; yes, we all know that the youngster is fumbling and the business may be lost, but he has to practise and if you do the job for him, he will never learn. This time *you* have the notebook to help you remember points and to advise him of his mistakes afterwards – and the things he did well! The client may find it surprising that you leave the work to your younger colleague, and he won't be particularly pleased if he feels that he is being used for training purposes. So you have to make an excuse to the client to explain why you are there and not contributing. If he doesn't know you, the best answer is that you have only recently joined the hotel and are getting to know the ropes, or that you are just visiting from out of town, or have laryngitis. Some excuse is needed. The crunch comes if you can see that you will lose the business if you don't interrupt. Then it is legitimate to do so, but you must wait until the last minute to give your pupil the best chance of completing the sale on his own. He still might get over his problems with the client if you give him a little more time, and senior men have to recognise that it is foolish to break in early on a 'Move over, son, and let a professional deal with it' basis.

The advantage of training an assistant personally is that you can deal with his individual problems, whereas in a training session with a group, you are much more likely to be speaking generally. The disadvantage is that whereas there is usually documentation attached to a training course, to enable the delegate to remember what he has been taught, on a personal basis this is usually absent. Yet it is no use hoping that a young salesman will remember everything; he has to have *aides memoire* as well. If you want him to carry out the appropriate market research when he talks to the client, he must have a check-list of what items you want covered. Just as every hotel has a Banquet Enquiry Sheet, so the salesman needs one to ensure that he has not forgotten anything.

In formal training sessions with a group, one of the most useful ways of bringing home technique in detail is to have someone act as the client while a delegate acts as the salesman. Ask the audience to observe the way the inter-view is conducted in order to suggest how the job could have been done better. The 'interview' need go on for only a few minutes at a time but the observations take much longer to cover, to point out all the things the sales-man did right and those that went wrong – some of which he might never have observed. For example, when a salesman is nervous, he tends to twiddle with a pen, pull out paper clips, rub his hands or regularly smooth down his hair. He will be unaware of these nervous mannerisms until they are pointed out. If you can stretch to closed-circuit TV with a playback, so much the better, but such expensive equipment is not essential. The audience observes and comments and, of course, the delegates are often reassured to see that other people make the same mistakes or that selling is not quite as difficult as it looks.

A good way to teach selling is to give each delegate in turn, playing the part of the salesman, a sample letter of enquiry from a client. The delegates in the audience have a copy, together with a list outlining what is in the client's mind. The task of the salesman acting out a first interview with the client is to identify the facts on the second sheet. If a letter of enquiry talks of a meeting room, the second sheet might identify the need for overnight accommodation and a dinner, which is also part of the exercise. If the salesman fails to elicit the information the audience already knows about, the lesson of market research comes home very strongly.

As good selling is so much a matter of practice, time should be found for the banqueting department and the other management concerned to make telephone calls to obtain further business. The best way of supervising the effectiveness of these calls is to listen in on another telephone line. It is very difficult to appreciate the quality of a sales presentation if you can hear only the salesman's end of it, and an extension line is therefore very important. The trainer should try to be out of sight of the salesman. It is difficult enough to sell, without feeling that there is somebody observing you, even with the best intentions. Try to have the type of extension where you can hear but not be heard. Helping with telephone selling is time-consuming; the client might not be in, he might be engaged. Even so, telephone selling is so important a part of the process, that time needs to be found for supervision in this area.

Selecting clients on which salesmen can practise is never easy. One useful source is all those clients who came a few years ago and have not been heard of since. The worst that can happen then, if the salesman does a poor job, is that you will continue not to see them. The clients are bound to be impressed that they have not been forgotten, and who knows – you might get a piece of business you did not expect.

As a small child I loathed being told that practice makes perfect, but of course, it is absolutely true, and selling is no exception. Flexibility, fluency and the confidence of experience only come with time and effort.

We have already discussed, in Chapter 2, the necessity to train both the telephonist and your secretary to handle incoming calls correctly. Most telephonists are conscientious and good at their jobs, but being G.P.O.-trained, they tend to treat all callers alike. You want to ensure that some outgoing calls are treated with particular care too – and I am not referring only to those from the Manager's extension!

When a conference client is in the hotel, the telephonist should be told which is his personal extension, and the extension of the room he is using for the meeting. These should be marked on the switchboard with a small label so that the telephonist is automatically alerted when one of these V.I.P. lines want service. Each day the telephonist should get a list of V.I.P. lines from the management, and should adjust the labels accordingly. There should be adequate supervision to ensure that everybody in that vital telephone room understands exactly what the policy is. No matter how hard a Banqueting Manager works to cover every detail to his client's satisfaction, no matter how good the food served in the restaurant, if a conference client has to interrupt a session for several minutes while he hangs on waiting for a call, his business is going to be that much harder to secure for the following year.

Communication between management and the restaurant staff is vital, too, so that they recognise important conference or other banqueting clients – perhaps dining in the restaurant the night before a conference or exhibition opens – and are aware when management or more junior staff are entertaining a client to a meal. This aspect is fully dealt with in the following chapter.

There is now a full range of films available, covering all aspects of sales training, and these are designed to be as pertinent to the hotel industry as any other. They range from American training films made in the 1950s with two excellent teachers called Borden and Bussey, to present-day productions featuring John Cleese and other TV favourites. The various subjects covered are a great help to anyone who wants to instil training in his staff, but isn't necessarily trained himself in the art. The films are available from companies like Rank and Video Arts Ltd.

Because there is a fair amount of staff turnover in hotels, it is very important to remember to contribute to the team effort. It is no use trying to excuse a blunder with the explanation that the member of staff involved only started a few days ago. The client is not interested. When somebody starts a job they are given basic instructions, but these do not usually include all the sales aspects that they should. What is more, the experience they have had in past jobs is probably weak in the sales area or, which is worse, they have been taught bad habits. It is important, therefore, to give instructions on how to behave in sales situations to new staff, porters and telephonists alike, so that they do the job correctly from the beginning. Then they will never have the excuse that 'I wasn't told . . .' which is just as damaging.

It is inevitable that people being trained are going to make mistakes. There are two vital aspects to mistakes: one, that they are brought to your attention; two, the way you deal with them. Some people try to push mistakes under the carpet, to pretend that they were not responsible, or that the mistakes did not even happen. The main reason for this behaviour is, of course, that they are afraid of the consequences. It is, therefore, very important that you make it as easy as possible for people to admit shortcomings, and that you deal with them as gently as possible. We have already established that selling is a hard skill to master, and the able executive is going to be doing his best without needing any spur from you. What he needs is information and guidance. What he does not need is sarcasm and to be made to look foolish, particularly in front of others. It is best therefore, to tell everybody in advance that mistakes are inevitable, and more helpful still if you can give instances where you made the same error yourself. You can also take the blame for a mistake by saying that you should have remembered to point out to the salesman the particular sales technique required. Let him down gently, encourage him, try always to correct him in private, and keep an eye on the progress he is making. A captain of industry was asked on his retirement if he would have changed anything in his business life if he had his time over again. The great man answered that the only alteration he would have made would have been to praise people more.

Remember to keep an eye on the letters which are being sent out by others in the sales area, but do not insist on signing them all yourself, and do not hold them up for too long. If corrections have to be made, the letter should still go out under the signature of the man who did the selling.

The concept of sales training might be quite new in your hotel, so there will be a great deal to do to get the attitude and standard up to scratch. The comforting thought as you tackle all this new work is that the standard is low in most hotels and few people are bothering to do much about it. You can be ahead of the field!

7
Entertaining

If a client is planning a function for which he expects the bill to come to hundreds of pounds, the decision on which hotel to use is not going to be taken lightly. This is particularly true if you are trying to persuade him to change from his previous venue. A good sales presentation takes a long time to carry out effectively, and you do not want interruptions. It is often not possible to hold a client's full attention on the telephone, and as we are talking about a discussion which might well take over an hour, a telephone call is hardly the answer. This is the occasion to invite the client to have lunch with you in the hotel.

The concept of selling over lunch is simple enough on the face of it: the client arrives, you have ample time to make a full presentation in amenable surroundings, and at the end of the meal, when the client has seen the hotel on its best behaviour, the booking is made in an atmosphere of everlasting friendship. Only a wild optimist would believe it to be that easy. We have already dealt with the actual sales presentation in detail in Chapter 3. But what of the meal itself? Many people, particularly young salesmen, are worried about entertaining. What is the right way of going about it in detail? What happens if, through nervousness, you dry up? Can a young manager logically entertain somebody as important as the managing director of a big company? It is essential to train staff to know in advance exactly what is involved in all aspects of entertaining correctly, so that mistakes do not occur. Slovenly attention to detail in the service of a meal itself can be just as disastrous as glaring errors in the sales presentation. The two go hand in hand, and it is the salesman's job to attend to his guest's every need, while still keeping up the momentum of his sales presentation. That is the purpose of this chapter.

Before the salesman meets the client at the hotel, there are a number of preliminary points to check. Firstly, why are you lunching the client at all?

How to Sell Banquets

You need a check-list of all the questions you want to ask him. Remember that the client is capable of giving you not only his own business, but possibly leads to other types of business as well. He might know one or two colleagues who have the responsibility for organising old boys' dinners, Masonic ladies' nights, regimental reunions and so on. If you ask him, he will almost certainly be glad to give you the names of the contacts; the more clients you ask, the more additional business you will find.

Secondly, check that you have your presentation book with you, and any tariffs or accommodation brochures you might need – and, of course, your notebook. You cannot concentrate on making your guest relaxed and at ease if your mind is obviously wandering to something vital you have suddenly realised that you have forgotten to bring.

You are now ready to meet the client. We have already discussed the correct treatment by the porter when he arrives. The porter is the host until you appear. But, of course, as you are expecting the client, there is a far better way to deal with his reception. Be there yourself. I have waited a total of probably weeks by now for clients to arrive: a quarter of an hour here, half an hour there, even an hour on occasions. But I have waited because that first impression is vital. Mess it up, and you are off on the wrong foot. I do not enjoy waiting for clients. Indeed it irritates me so much that I refuse to wait for anybody in my private life. But from the salesman's point of view, the client who is late puts himself at a considerable disadvantage. He arrives late and finds the salesman patiently waiting. He apologises and the salesman assures him that it does not matter at all, making some feeble excuse that he had other work to do anyway, and brushing aside the apology as quite unnecessary. Most clients would now like to make a gesture of thanks for this courtesy. What can it be? The most usual form it takes is to pay more than normal attention to what the salesman is saying; to start in a positive frame of mind to consider the salesman's proposals. This is exactly what you want to achieve, so a good salesman actually hopes the client will be at least a little late.

But what normally happens? By some gesture, deliberate or accidental, the amateur salesman communicates his irritation to the client. He might reply to the apology that the traffic was very bad with the cutting remark, 'It always is at this time of day'. The words are innocuous enough, but the inflection can be highly critical: people shouldn't keep others waiting; it is rude and thoughtless. The customer gets annoyed and the atmosphere cools rapidly. The salesman, however, is interested in getting more business, not in correcting the manners of clients. You can make the client feel small and lose the business. Never forget that, in selling, there is always a great danger of winning battles and losing wars.

You hear the client give his name to the porter. You step forward to greet him, and from this moment on your dual role as host and salesman begins.

You will probably offer the client a drink in the bar before lunch, ushering him into the bar ahead of you and suggesting a seat which gives him a wide view. Try to seat yourself to one side so that you are in no way boxing him in – he is not your prisoner and must not be made to feel so. Always face the client. Never sit beside him in the bar or on a banquette in the restaurant. You have to be able to observe him closely at all times in order to analyse his reactions.

It is easy enough to know his reaction if he says, 'I don't like that suggestion,' or 'I don't want to pay that much,' but clients are often less frank. They do not want to appear to be bargaining with you; they don't want to abuse their position as your guest, and they don't want to get into an argument. Very often, therefore, you cannot judge unfavourable reactions from what the client says. You have to judge from what he does, from his body movements. If that sounds difficult, let us start with some simple examples. What do you do when you are bored? Some people drum their fingers on the desk, some gaze vacantly at the ceiling, some shift their positions more often than normal. You can usually recognise boredom. What is perhaps less easy to interpret is the act of folding the arms; this very often happens when people dislike the opinion they have just heard. They are shutting it out. If a client folds his arms, I immediately mentally check what I have just said. A slight frown on the client's forehead would be more helpful, but suddenly folded arms is a clue you must not miss. Say something the client does not like, and he might move his chair backwards, away from you, shift uncomfortably, tighten his lips, or narrow and harden his eyes. If he wants to interrupt, he will obviously open his mouth; allow him to stop you when he wants to contribute.

Watch your guest at all times. If he looks round in the bar, he might be wondering why there are no nuts or crisps on his table, when the guests across the room have some. If he is to regard himself as an important guest of the management, he is at least entitled to the same titbits as anybody else. If the bartender omits to check that there is no liquid on the base of the glass when the drinks arrive, you must do it.

Now how should the conversation proceed? If the client is going to be with you for, say, an hour and a half, how much of that time should be spent talking business? As much as you can possibly cram in. I did not learn that lesson for many years, and as a consequence I have a smattering of knowledge of tea planting in Nepal in the 1920s, a first-hand account of being shot down over France in the First World War, an eye-witness description of the great Tokyo earthquake, and many other fascinating snippets. What I do not have is as much information as I might about the occasions when companies use hotels.

How to Sell Banquets

I am often asked whether it is polite to talk business all the time if you invite people to lunch. Wouldn't it be more courteous to make small talk about children or holidays, hobbies or the state of the nation? I think it is more discourteous to do so than to talk business. To make small talk is to suggest that the client can waste the time he has granted you to talk business. His business should be very important to him; after all, you would not welcome small talk if he had come for a meeting in your office, or you had gone to his office. A degree of small talk will enter into the conversation inevitably, but for the great majority of the time, stick to business.

You will offer your guest another drink, and if he declines, you will ask him if he would now like to go into lunch. You will usher him to the restaurant beside or in front of you, depending on the width of the corridor – never behind you – and the Restaurant Manager will lead you to your table. Your client will follow the Restaurant Manager and you will bring up the rear.

You should, of course, have booked the table in advance, selecting just the one you want. Choose a round table, not a banquette, so that you can face your guest, and make sure that you are given one in a quiet position, perhaps against a wall but not too near the kitchen or entrance doors. You do not want your sales presentation to have to compete more than is necessary with the coming and going of normal restaurant service. The Restaurant Manager should offer your guest the seat with the better view of the room, leaving the one with a restricted view for you.

It is up to you to make sure in advance that the restaurant staff know that you are entertaining an important business client. Their service should always be good, but it must be even better on this occasion. This is particularly important when it is not the Banqueting Manager but a more junior member of the team who is entertaining a client. If the restaurant staff have not been told the facts in advance, what they see is a comparatively junior member of the staff apparently living it up in a manner to which they would all like to become accustomed. The fact that he is entertaining a potential customer and apt to get indigestion from nervousness with every mouthful is less apparent; and it is possible that the salesman – and more important his client – will not get good service. It must therefore be explained in advance that the service has to be first class, not for the sake of the member of staff, but for his guest and for the sake of the business he might bring in.

So now you are sitting down. The first thing to do is to check that the client has a napkin and a bread roll, if there are rolls for all the guests. When the menu arrives, the waiter will normally give it to you first because he recognises a member of the management. It is really a waste of time to point out year after year that guests are served first, even in the matter of menus, so the best thing is simply to pass it on to the client as if you were a postman delivering the waiter's messages. As soon as the menu is brought, there are a number of points to remember. Most menus include both the *table d'hôte* and the *à la carte* selections, and the client is going to wonder exactly what he is being offered. To settle any doubt in his mind, you should immediately recommend one or two dishes from the *à la carte* menu, to show him that he can choose anything he likes. Never skimp on a client's entertaining. If he is not important enough to entertain as well as possible, then he should not be there in the first place.

The appearance of a menu cluttered up with kitchen French can be intimidating. Most menus nowadays have explanations for the French names, but these are often omitted on the *table d'hôte*. Sometimes they are not to be found on the *à la carte*, either. To put a client at his ease, you should suggest those dishes without explanations and gently explain them as you go along. Invite him to help by saying something like, 'Now what would that be? White wine and tomato, I suppose,' and grumbling slightly, 'I would like to see hotels give up these old-fashioned practices, but so many of the clients still seem to like them'. This is not true, but what can you do if you are stuck with a piece of promotional material that makes the client look an idiot because he cannot understand it?

Here it is necessary for you to be able to distinguish between the unsophisticated client, where help is probably necessary, and the sophisticated one, where it might be considered patronising. In such cases you can flatter the client by saying, 'I won't recommend dishes to somebody with your experience. I'm sure you have your favourites. What can I offer you?' If you can persuade the client to order his favourite dishes, the likelihood of his enjoying his meal is obviously greater, so you must try to encourage him to tell you what they are. Some people are embarrassed at a liking for snails or fish and chips, and need reassuring that a taste for garlic or simple dishes is perfectly acceptable.

The wine waiter should, of course, offer you the wine list, as the host. Again you will have to assess the degree of experience of the client before you ask, 'Red or white?' of the unsophisticated, and 'A glass of claret or Burgundy?' of the more knowledgable. Always say 'a glass'. It is important to avoid the impression so well illustrated in a cartoon by Peter Arno, in which there was a particularly dizzy blonde on a bar stool, and her boy-friend was saying to the bar tender, 'Fill 'er up'. You are going to order a bottle, but you are offering a glass. The client will drink as much or as little as he wants, but the hospitality will not be meagre.

Throughout the meal you have to watch for absentees: croûtons, mustard, the correct sauce, all the vegetables the client ordered, enough butter, the right cutlery and so on. The client is not to be embarrassed by having to ask, and you don't want the service of the hotel to look slipshod in the absence of essentials. If your guest starts to look round the restaurant when he should be starting to eat, it will almost certainly mean that the mint sauce to accompany his lamb has not been offered. Of course it is the waiter's responsibility to see that this does not happen. But you must be on the alert, too, and ask for it before your guest even notices that it is lacking.

If by this point you are wondering how you are ever going to enjoy your own lunch whilst ensuring in such minute detail that the client is enjoying his, the answer is that it does not matter if you don't. The purpose of entertaining is not for you to enjoy a meal; it is to obtain a piece of business. When I see a salesman tucking into his lunch as the client glances anxiously around for the water he ordered – and remember that some Europeans do like to drink mineral water with their wine – I always recognise an amateur. Indeed, the professional salesman usually eats very lightly. He is going to do a substantial part of the presentation during lunch, and the market research for other business as well. To try to eat an enormous meal at the same time plays havoc with one's digestion over a period of time. And it is rude to talk with your mouth full! Better to order a light soup to start, perhaps cold meat and salad, and to forego a dessert. It might appear a Spartan repast, but your stomach will show its gratitude by giving you no trouble afterwards!

One of your problems is going to be to correct any serious errors of service as discreetly as possible. There was one occasion when an inexperienced wine waiter brought the red wine in an ice bucket. Luckily the client did not notice, so I simply removed it and pointed out to the waiter that, as it was not too warm a day, we would not use the ice bucket on this occasion! But needless to say, the wine waiter learned a little from the rocket afterwards, and probably never did it again.

Everybody in the hotel team, from the porter and the telephonist, to the complete restaurant staff play their part in bringing off a sale, and because of this they must all be taught the importance of their role. A sale can be lost at any point because of the weakness of any one member. It once took me two years to get a client to lunch in order to see a hotel, and eventually I persuaded him to come. He ordered *Lobster Newburg*, and very properly the Maitre d'hotel told him that it would take 25 minutes to prepare. The client was quite happy to wait, and I surreptitiously kept an eye on my watch and hoped all would go well. Twenty-five minutes and then thirty minutes passed, and the client was getting impatient. Then, at long last, up came *Lobster Americain!* It took me another two years to get that particular conference. On the other hand, I am sure that one major function was obtained as much as anything because of the elegant and professional way in which a Turkish waiter prepared a *Steak Tartare* for my client at the table.

There has to be a rapport built up between the Restaurant Manager, or a specific waiter, and the salesman, so that the service is planned in advance. By planning, I mean that it should be absolutely efficient, but not obtrusive. There is nothing worse than reaching the culminating point in a sales presentation and then having the waiter come up and enquire, 'Is everything all right?' The flow is stopped, the spell is broken and the waiter can have cost you whatever the sale was worth. Decision-making time is not to be interrupted under any circumstances. Equally, the Maitre d'hotel who feels like taking the opportunity of chatting with a member of the management has to be warned in advance that there are more important things to be done. When you are selling, you don't want any but the absolutely essential interruptions, which are basically to take the order and then come back again for the choice of dessert.

You should tell the staff in advance that you will be offering your guest liqueurs and cigars, so that the waiter comes to the table at just the right time to take the order. Again, it is a small cost to show the client a standard of entertaining which clearly spares no expense to please him.

It is, of course, necessary to train other members of management in the art of selling when entertaining, but it is important not to take more than one of them with you at a time. The client all by himself with three members of the opposition surrounding him, feels at a disadvantage, and will put up more resistance to buying. He feels intimidated by sheer numbers. Also, he is far more difficult to shift from a position once he has stated it in front of such an audience. If he says he thinks the dance floor is too small, he is more likely to be persuaded away from that view if there is only one salesman than if he has made the statement to three or four.

There are occasions when you have two clients coming to lunch together; for example, there can be a Sales Administration Manager who actually has to do all the work for the conference, and a Sales Director who has to agree to which venue to use. The sales presentation will be to both of them, but they are obviously going to wish to consult with each other before making a final decision. If you do not give them the opportunity during their time with you – and that means leaving them so that they can confer in private – they will have to do so after they have left you. That means that they will leave the hotel without having made up their minds and, in your absence, doubts could be allowed to creep in and spoil the effect of your sales presentation. Do not let this happen. When you have completed your sales presentation, and have asked them whether they would like to raise any other questions, make an excuse to leave them for a couple of minutes – to greet another guest in the restaurant, to check a point in the hotel banqueting book, a detail on the banquet menu, or any other excuse you like. Then when you return, be prepared to ask for the business. More sales are lost at this point than at any other time.

Never be afraid to make notes. It is not considered discourteous even when you are entertaining a client. The client wants to be sure that you have noted all the small details accurately, and he cannot reasonably expect you to remember them all.

When the lunch is over, usher the clients out ahead of you. Do not bid them farewell in the lobby. Take them outside and be sure that they are either heading in the right direction down the street towards their next destination, or being conveyed off in their means of transport before considering your job is over for the time being. If they need a taxi, wait until it comes. If they say, 'Don't worry; we'll find one,' or 'Don't stand out here in the cold,' pay no attention. Until they are safely away, your task is not completed. You have done everything up to this point to ensure that they have been looked after properly. Don't spoil the ship for a hap'orth of tar.

In this chapter we have discussed the technicalities of entertaining. These should be clearly understood and so well known to the salesman that they become reflex actions, something that he can cope with automatically whilst concentrating on his sales presentation. Perhaps it would be a help to look upon the entertaining as the orchestra playing the background music to the performance of the solo singer.

8

Letter Construction

In the chapter on the early stages of selling banquets, I pointed out that the letter is not a favoured sales weapon. There are occasions, however, when you cannot sell in person to a client, and there are very often occasions when he asks for details in writing, in order to show the possibilities to his colleagues. In subsequent years when the client has already seen the hotel, the letter may also be all he asks for because he has not the time to visit you. Writing banqueting letters is not difficult, but many people make it seem so by failing to accept certain principles. These are:

1. There is only one English language. There are not two, one for talking and one for writing. Every letter is simply the spoken word down on paper.

2. Not all hoteliers speak English as their mother tongue. You probably speak a number of other languages, and I have always been embarrassed that I speak only the one. So, if English is not your best language, don't tackle the grammar and phrasing of the letters yourself. Let somebody whose English is perfect put your thoughts into words because otherwise you are likely to fail to communicate as you would wish.

You will remember the apocryphal letter from a continental hotelier which read in part, 'Each room has a magnificent view over the gorge. We hope you drop in'. You are likely to drop in too if you don't ask for help. I know that many hoteliers will not adopt this suggestion because they will feel it involves a loss of face. But the alternative of sending out poor letters will make you look much more foolish in the eyes of every half-literate client; so it's the devil and the deep blue sea. If your manager is making this mistake, it is a kindness to point it out.

3. The letter you send has to be just as credible as you would be in a personal interview.

4. The points we have discussed in the chapter on promotional material

(Chapter 4) apply to letters as well. Ensure that they are not going to arrive crumpled, folded badly or sloppily typed.

Let us first of all tackle the point about there being only one English language. Would you believe that there are still hotels 'assuring you of my best attention at all times'? A lot of letters still end with this phrase, yet do you honestly believe when you read those words that the writer is sincere? Do you believe him when he promises to give you all the attention you could possibly want? It is far more likely that you consider it in the same way as the phrase 'your sincerely'. It is a platitude, a cliché, and it carries no conviction at all. The writer might very well give you good attention, but when he 'assures you' of it, the phrase completely loses any meaning. The result will probably be that you won't believe him for a moment. Never fall into this trap yourself. Do not use this phrase and do not use any other phrase you constantly see churned out in business letters. Do not 'beg' to acknowledge, 'herewith' enclose, or 'duly' receive. All business English is bad because it is stilted and appears insincere, even though it may not be.

Exactly the same applies to superlatives. The public today has been deluged, swamped and all but drowned in a sickening flood of over-exaggeration in advertising. Everything is wonderful, everything is better than ever before, new, practically free, bigger, the greatest or the most. Words like 'magnificent', 'gorgeous', 'finest' or 'superb' have an effect only if applied to detergents. The public would probably expect a detergent that wasn't advertised as 'the whitest' to make clothes dirtier than ever before. This illustrates the danger you run if in your letter, you praise the product to the skies. The client might well have confidence in you, but he will wince as he tries to explain to a committee that you are far more credible in person than you are on paper. Most people simply don't believe wild promises, and they are not necessary.

Don't gild the lily either. If you have just put in air conditioning, do not describe it as 'superb air conditioning'. Either it works or it doesn't work. 'Effective air conditioning' is what the client wants to read, because that solves his problem of smoke and humidity. So do not suggest in your letter that you can supply an impossibly high standard, any more than you would claim that to him in person. 'Good', 'fine', 'lovely', 'pretty' and 'first class' are still words that have some meaning, but the clients won't believe much more than that.

Many people still find it hard to accept the point I made, that the letter is the spoken word put down on paper. I read a lot of letters over the course of a year, and while those I receive from friends at home give me an instant impression of their personalities, the business letters could easily be programmed by computers for the use of severely introverted robots. No impression of the writer comes through at all. Many people still believe that there is a language – Business English – specially designed for use in business letters. Nothing could be further from the truth. 'Business English' was originally a collection of phrases which an illiterate man could use to disguise the fact that he was illiterate, and therefore couldn't write the language correctly.

The famous letter-writers in our literature were able, because they had time to think, to produce similies, metaphors, elaborate phrases, a flow of words and a logical progression of ideas. These often put their letters in a higher literary class than their conversation: a playwright is usually more coherent on paper than when he is making a speech off the cuff. But whether spoken or written, the language is the same. If I said to a client, 'assuring you of my best attention at all times', he would probably think I was drunk! Read your own letters and see whether you would have spoken the words you have written down. It is amazing how many hoteliers with engaging personalities, a large vocabulary and a ready wit, become zombies as soon as they start to write letters. When the client gets a set of letters from suppliers offering ballrooms and menus, the one which invokes an individual and natural personality is certainly going to stand out amongst the dross of 'I am enclosing for your perusal . . . .'.

Another excellent way of giving the impression to the client that you have ceased to regard him as a friend and are writing to him strictly on business, is the popping in of the odd word in Latin. 'Per person', as against 'a guest', is the prime example. And as we are talking of the guests, never use the word 'persons' in this way – 'I note that you are expecting 120 persons'. 'Persons' are arrested for shoplifting; we deal with guests, delegates, visitors, but never persons.

Although your letters should be grammatical, they should also be reasonably colloquial. The reader will not recognise the style in which you talk if you become grammatically stilted when you write. If you would say 'don't', you should not write 'do not'. Grammatically you are not supposed to start letters with 'and' or 'but', and 'however' should not come earlier in a sentence than the third word or later than the fifth or sixth. But such rules are unnecessary; you are not trying to pass an English examination, but to communicate a warm and friendly personality. Stop to consider this: have you been trying to communicate a warm and friendly personality? I am afraid it is more likely that you have been trying to impress the clients with the status and respectability of your hotel or to produce a letter which will fool them about your inexperience in writing letters.

What about our industry's jargon? We talk of 'cash bars', 'pre-dinner drinks', 'classroom fashion', 'on consumption' and many other phrases which are a shorthand to us. But they can grate on the customer, even if he under-stands what they mean – which is by no means guaranteed. The worst exam-ple of jargon is, of course, the French menu itself, but we have dealt with that already. We are not alone, by any means, in using jargon, as anybody who has tried to get his car repaired, his TV fixed, or even buy a cooker, will readily agree. What jargon does convey to the customer, though, is that there are some of us who are insiders and then there is you, the customer, who is an outsider because you don't speak the language. That is quite simply the wrong message to put over. It creates a barrier between ourselves and the guests, which is exactly what we want to avoid. So it is best, wherever poss-ible, to refrain from using jargon in your letters.

A word about the lay-out of letters. The paper on which your letter is typed should be considered as a frame for the typing and heading. The letter should be in the middle of the paper with margins on both sides, and a border top and bottom. Apart from the fact that this arrangement makes the letter easier to read, the symmetry is attractive in itself, and gives an impression of order and organisation. A letter spread across the paper in a haphazard man-ner with no attempt at margins on the right side, or cramped into the top third of the paper, looks as amateur as a cross bat on a cricket field. And it goes without saying that any errors must be neatly erased, or the letter retyped.

In an attempt to make letters look individual, many hotels use a coloured typewriter ribbon, or a coloured paper which is common to all their station-ery. There are benefits in adopting – and keeping – a distinctive coloured paper, typeface, or envelope, in that your letter is instantly recognisable and stands out in a crowd. A letter from you to a regular client should be like a beacon of warmth and friendship amidst the rocks of business negotiations.

We have a technique in selling which is known as 'you appeal'. It needs a little explanation. Why are you reading this book? To feed my children? To support a worthy publisher? To keep the paper trade in caviare? No, you are reading it for the benefit you believe it might have for you. You are interested in your own problems, and why not? So are most people. When you read a letter, you remain interested in your own problems, and when the letter talks of 'you' and 'yours', it really talks your language. When it talks of 'us', 'we' and 'ours', it interests you far less. If we don't recognise this fact, there is a tendency to write letters with far too many 'we's' and far too few 'you's'. Look at some of the letters you have written recently and see how you could have changed the wording to reflect the interests of your client better. There are two letters illustrated here; one shows how the letter might have been writ-ten, if thought were not given to the principle (Fig. 5), and the other has 'you appeal' (Fig. 6).

Letter with indirect approach

Dear Mr. Gibbons,

　　Further to my call yesterday, I am now
enclosing our sample menus for the dinner on
March 9th. I have made a note that 70 guests
are now expected, and we will be providing a
full bar before dinner.

　　I am also enclosing our banqueting wine list.
I should be grateful if we could learn of the
wines selected in time to print the menus about a
month before the dinner.

　　I have told our florist to get in touch with
Mrs. Gibbons to discuss the floral decorations,
and we will do all we can to ensure that the
dinner is a great success.

　　　　　　　　　　　Yours sincerely,

　　　　　　　　　　　Manager,
　　　　　　　　　　　King William Hotel

Figure 5. There are 13 'I', 'we' or 'our's' in this letter, and sending it could be unlucky too!

Letter with 'you appeal'

Dear Mr. Gibbons,

You said on the 'phone yesterday that you'd like some sample menus and these you will find enclosed with this letter. A note has been made that you are now expecting 70 guests and a full bar will be available before dinner as you asked.

You will also find the banqueting wine list enclosed, and it would be a help if you could choose the wines you want a month before the dinner so that the printing can be done in good time.

The florist will be getting in touch with your wife to discuss the floral decorations and you can be certain that everything will be done to ensure that your dinner is a great success.

Yours sincerely,

Manager,
King William Hotel

Figure 6. Now there are 11 'you' and 'your's', and no 'I', 'we' or 'our's'. Nothing much else has changed except the feeling of the letter.

Let us have a look at the type of letter which should achieve the best results when received (Fig. 7A, B). You will see first that it is addressed to Arthur Robinson, rather than A. Robinson. It is another part of the process of establishing a first-name relationship. The purpose of the budget, as mentioned in the first paragraph is to save him from working out the figures for himself. If you get a tender from a supplier, you expect it to itemise the expenditure rather than tell you, for example, that a decorator will use 27½ gallons of paint at a cost to you of £8.49 a gallon, and leave you to work out what that comes to as a total. One of the main dangers that has to be avoided with a budget is to have it rejected as too high, so the first paragraph leaves you with an escape clause that the figure can be adjusted if necessary. The phrase 'on the high side' is an example of a colloquialism that adds to the letter's credibility simply because it it colloquial. 'A way will be found round the problem' is a positive declaration that you can be relied upon even when the crunch comes.

In the second paragraph we are homing in on the factor of prime importance for the evening: that the Production Director should enjoy himself at his own retirement dinner. He likes duck and so we offer duck in a large variety of ways. Our expertise in cooking duck is thereby illustrated. Notice the word 'stunning'. It is a word which has impact in this context, where 'large' for instance would be dull and lifeless as an alternative. We establish our expertise further by discounting *Caneton à l'Anglaise* as a poor banqueting dish for considerable numbers and we manage a touch of humour in using the word 'pro-Europeans'; *Caneton à l'Anglaise,* instead of Roast Duck, is an affectation. When we excuse it by saying that we are pro-Europeans, the stupidity of the excuse makes it clear that we are laughing at ourselves. It makes the hotel more human, less overwhelming.

In the third paragraph there are more suggestions for making the event special for Mr Tisdale. We do not, however, just assume that the client is made of money and doesn't care about the cost. In suggesting the silk-screen printed menus, we acknowledge 'that is a lot of money for a napkin' and remind Mr Robinson that we want to take care of his expenditure. There are four 'I's' and 'we's' on page one, to eight 'you's' and 'your's'.

The first paragraph on page two continues with customer benefits, and since there is an apposite story to tell of another retirement dinner, it is included. Again it makes you look more human, it is unusual – because how many times does a business letter tell stories? – and it makes one other important point; your hotel is good enough to be chosen by Unilever for an event of this nature. You are not saying that if it is good enough for Unilever, it ought to be good enough for Mr Tisdale, but Mr Robinson will be able to add two and two together as well as the next man. You also point out that the client is

THE KING
WILLIAM

The King William Hotel
Cathedral Square, Barchester S4U 3WS
Telephone: (0998) 121 5661 Telex: 123456 Cables: DOMESDAY

September 30th

Arthur Robinson Esq.,
Walker & Smith Limited,
13 High Street,
MIDDLECOMBE

Dear Mr. Robinson,

    I have made a provisional booking for you for the
Hastings Room on December 10th, and you will find attached
a draft budget which itemises your total expenditure. If,
of course, the final figure comes out on the high side, do
let me know and a way will be found around the problem.

    You explained over the telephone that the object of the
dinner was to mark the retirement of your Production
Director, and there is no difficulty in serving his
favourite, duck, as the main course. It can be prepared plain
or in a stunning variety of garnishes - orange, black cherry,
with green Spanish olives, with peaches, pineapple, or
perhaps he has a particular favourite which could be prepared
for him specially. As you know, it is easier to serve 100
people with duck to a high standard if there is a sauce, so I
don't really recommend Caneton à l'Anglaise as we pro-Europeans
put it.

    Do you like the idea of having all the rolls that evening
in the shape of 'S' as his name is Steven? It doesn't cost
any more, and you might also like to consider as a souvenir
of the occasion silk-screening the menus on to the napkins.
This makes a very attractive table decoration, though they do
cost about 75p each. That is a lot of money for a napkin, but
it is difficult to find as inexpensive a memento of the event.

As the colours of your company are blue and gold, you
might like to have blue and gold carnations for floral
decorations. If you are going to make a presentation, please
let me know you need to keep it hidden until the right moment.
I remember we had some difficulty a few years ago when one
of the Unilever Directors retired, and it was decided to give
him a contribution to his retirement hobby - two live sheep!
Still, we got them safely into the banqueting room and I
doubt whether you will have anything more difficult than that.

You will notice that I have suggested Christmas Pudding,
and whilst it is perfectly true that a lot of it gets eaten
at Christmas-time, on December 10th it will probably be the
first time in the year that anyone has tasted it. I know
your own fondness for it, and if you are doing all the work,
you could perhaps give yourself this small indulgence.

You will see from the budget that the cost of cigars
has not been included and, of course, you are very welcome
to bring your own if you so wish. The price of Havanas
continues to soar, but one interesting development recently
is that the Jamaicans have found a new source of wrapper
leaf in the Cameroons and are using it for a brand called
Royal Jamaica. These are substantially cheaper than Havanas
and if you let me know what size you think appropriate, I
can give you a quotation.

I fully appreciate the affection you all have for Mr.
Tisdale and you can be quite certain that if you decide to
use the hotel, everything possible will be done to ensure
that he has a truly memorable evening. When you have had the
time to mull over the letter and quotation, I will give you
a ring and see whether a date can be arranged for you to
come to the hotel and discuss the other details. Why not
come for lunch? I know how busy you are, but you have to eat,
and Harry is practising his Bloody Mary's to get them
perfect for you next time.

With kind regards,

Yours sincerely,

Derek Taylor,
Manager,
King William Hotel

WALKER & SMITH LTD – RETIREMENT DINNER

FOR MR. STEVEN TISDALE

Hastings Room, King William Hotel:
Thursday, December 10th

Cocktail Reception – 30 minutes	200.00
100 Dinners @ £7.50	750.00
25 Bottles of Chablis 1976 @ £4.90	122.50
25 Bottles of Du Pape 1976 @ £4.70	117.50
Liqueurs or Brandy – 100 @ 70p	70.00
Table decorations – 10 @ £5.25	52.50
Toastmaster	40.00
Band	190.00
Band suppers – 4 @ £4.50	18.00
Total to include VAT and Service Charges	£1,560.50

Note: Please remember that this does not include the free bar after Dinner, menu printing, Cabaret, a bouquet for the ladies or cigarettes on the tables.

Figure 7A. Previous pages. Figure 7B (above): Budget for the Retirement Dinner

always right, even if he wants to bring in live sheep! Somewhere in your own hotel's experience there will be examples of how to put yourselves out in some particular way for a client, and you should use that instance to put over your message of fine service.

Paragraph 2 on that page acknowledges that Mr Robinson is working very hard, and you appreciate that, even if nobody else does. You are making the menu attractive to Mr Robinson and that will, hopefully, help to get his vote for the venue – not just the meal if it comes to a vote. The use of the phrase 'this small indulgence' is to excuse his own tastes taking preference over those of the guest of honour. The next paragraph makes the point again about the hotel's expertise and desire to save the client wasting his money. The final paragraph leaves the ball firmly in your court to take the next step, rather than wait for the client to react. Again there is a touch of humour in the Bloody Marys and the reassurance that you are fully aware of the importance of the evening. There are 24 'you's' this time, to 13 'I's' and 'we's'.

Of course this kind of letter takes a great deal more time to prepare than the normal 'am enclosing a selection of sample menus and our wine list' type. Too many hotels, however, consider that the menus speak for themselves, the wine list speaks for itself, and the client should come to the hotel because of all the good things the world will have told him about it. This is either a highly complacent attitude or delusions of grandeur. The letter can be a much more powerful selling aid if you take enough time with it.

The letter we have examined is, in no way, a formal, stylised document, but at the same time it is not the last word in personalised correspondence. There are many other ways in which you can make the client pick out your letter from the general run-of-the-mill offering. You can adopt some or all of the ideas which follow, or you can produce something special for yourself. For example the 'Dear' in 'Dear Mr Smith' is considered by a lot of people to be a bad start to a letter which seeks to be credible. They say it is foolish to suggest that we are as fond of every client as 'Dear' suggests. Consequently many people start business letters with, 'Thank you Mr Smith . . . for the letter you sent on August 10th' or, 'I'm grateful, Mr Smith . . . for the chance to quote for your dinner/dance'. Certainly if your letters start like that, the client is going to sit up and take notice. Another personalized touch is to use the name of the client more than once in your letter. Invariably the letter starts 'Dear Mr Smith', and the name of Mr Smith is never mentioned again. This is in spite of the already established fact that the man likes the sound of his own name. There is no reason why it should not be mentioned again. You may write at present, 'You can be certain that everything will be done to ensure the success of the dinner'. It sounds even better as, 'You can be certain, Mr Smith, that everything will be done to ensure the success of the dinner'.

How to Sell Banquets

Many people set out to write good, colloquial English and still find that the finished result reads almost as formally as ever. The brain-washing of their business education over the years seems constantly to drag them back into a formalised style. One main reason for this is the use of formal words where informal ones are readily available. The formal words which constantly creep in are words like 'requirements' when we could use 'needs', 'assistance' when we could use 'help', and 'facilities' when we could use 'rooms'. Compare the examples which follow.

1. 'If you would acquaint me with the facilities you have selected, I shall be glad to offer you every assistance, and your requirements will receive my personal attention.'
2. 'If you could let me know which rooms you would like, I'll do all I can to help.'

What you want to convey is the same in both cases, but the wording is very different. Many people believe that you can't write business letters with sentences like example 2. That there is a convention, a tradition, a company policy that collapses with consternation at the use of colloquial English. That the dignity and status of our organisation will be seriously undermined if we 'help' rather than 'assist' and deal with 'needs' rather than 'requirements'. I can only ask why this should be? And, furthermore, could someone tell me why dignity as against courtesy is the correct aim? Dignity is stuffy, appropriate for state occasions and little else; it is out of keeping with the times, boring and old-fashioned. Do not, however, confuse dignity with manners, courtesy or civilised behaviour. Those remain just as valid objectives as ever.

When writing, as in selling face-to-face, don't tell a client what he cannot have or cannot do unless you provide a reason and explanation. And consider whether you really are stopping him doing what he wants. Here is a simple example from any hotel. The sign reads, 'Personal cheques cannot be cashed without prior arrangement or without the production of a valid Bankers' Card'. You see these notices all over the place. But another way of putting it is, 'Personal cheques can be cashed by prior arrangement or by production of a valid Bankers' Card'. A negative restriction has turned into a positive service. 'We cannot get an extension beyond 1 o'clock,' reads much better as, 'We can get an extension up to 1 o'clock.' Think positively, and see whether the situation can be presented in a more encouraging manner. If you genuinely can't do what the client wants, remember that you are going to disappoint him, so make sure that he understands the situation clearly. Do not write, 'The absolute maximum number of guests you can have is 100', but, 'I have set up the room in every way I can think to try to fit in the 110 guests who have accepted your invitation, but with the best will in the world, the room will only seat 100. I'm terribly sorry because I appreciate the problems this will cause, but there really doesn't seem to be anything more we can do.'

It is only a small point, but I have always felt that continuation paper was a very mean invention. The fact that you are prepared to save a sheet of headed notepaper by the use of a continuation sheet hardly gives the client confidence that you will avoid similar short cuts with his service, the size of the portions or the quality of the *petits fours!* If you are prepared to save even a sheet of headed paper, what will you do to the number of flowers in the vase on the table.

Lastly, let me make one point again: when sending letters, don't forget to instruct your secretary very carefully how you want them folded and put in the envelopes. That beautiful, pristine appearance of the letter you signed can get as badly mauled before your client opens the envelope as any other material sent in a faulty envelope. Remember again that most secretaries do not fold letters properly unless they are carefully instructed. It is all too easy to do the job quickly and fractionally less than neatly.

I have already admitted that a salesman does not like using the letter as a major weapon if he can avoid it, but when it has to be used, it should be constructed with infinite care.

It Takes All Types . . .

In a just world the salesman who has a good product at a fair price, who makes a good presentation and is flexible in his approach, ought to get the business. Yet time and again salesmen find that this is not enough. They appear to do everything right and the client still doesn't buy. There is nothing so irritating, and the salesman goes over everything he has said in his mind afterwards, trying to work out what went wrong. Very often what went wrong can be summed up in one word; empathy. Empathy is the capacity to understand another person's mental processes and to act in sympathy with them. The buying process is affected by the client's psychological make-up to a greater or lesser extent. We are none of us automatons to make decisions like some opponent of Dr Who. We are human, have human failings and hang-ups and they matter. The primary motives – the price, location, service and so on – are often only the tip of the iceberg, but the secondary motives which we are going to discuss at length here are the mass beneath the surface.

You can assess the client's secondary motives in many ways; you can describe him as neurotic, full of complexes, prejudiced, radical or ultra-conservative. This is not, however, an exercise in deep psychological investigation; that is for professional medical practitioners, and our clients, hopefully, will seldom be in need of them. It is a much more elementary exercise in how to overcome the problems that the client doesn't raise when you are selling your product to him.

Let us take an example. Many customers feel that the atmosphere of a good hotel is overpowering. They might be given the responsibility for a staff party because it was their turn, and they might be quite overcome at the surroundings when they visit you. One of the first dinners I ever sold was for the foremen of a small international company. They had outgrown their canteen for the Christmas dinner so they had to move to a hotel. On the night, they arrived with their wives at what was really a very modest hotel. Yet during cocktail time they all practically stood to attention, afraid to speak, feeling desperately out of place, while the Managing Director tried desperately to get them to relax. After some drinks at that time and some more with the dinner, the atmosphere improved; but it took a very long time before the guests were enjoying themselves. Some years later, when they had been at the hotel for the same party each December, the Managing Director suggested a change and was surprised when there was unanimous opposition. The guests had finally got accustomed to the hotel and they had no wish to go through the experience of new intimidating surroundings again.

A lot of people are nervous of hotels to this day; they have to be reassured that the uniforms, the French dishes, the rows of knives and forks, the wine list and the other elements we take for granted are not beyond them. Such clients are inclined to choose the poorer value for money, the less elegant décor, the scruffier hotel because they feel more at home in it. Watch this problem with Trade Union clients, with members of organising committees from non-management jobs, with students and young charity committees. The inferiority complex sapping the confidence of the client can take business away from you.

How do you deal with it? By quite positively setting out to debunk all the hotel industry mystique. When talking of wine, say to the client, 'I don't know why they make such a fuss about wine lists. Nobody can tell one red from another anyway, and really it's just a question of whether you like sweet or dry.' Deal with French dishes and all the other jargon in the same way.

Everybody is prejudiced about something. There are people who dislike long hair, waistcoats, punk clothes, posh accents, foreigners and communists, amongst an endless list of other things. The salesman has to avoid all arguments with clients; you are a salesman, not a missionary. On one occasion I had a sales conference for a cosmetic house in my pocket and was getting on very well with their Sales Director. The subject at lunch shifted to sales recruitment, on which I have very strong views. They did not happen to coincide with the equally strongly-held beliefs of my client and within half an hour, between the main course and dessert, I had managed to antagonise him to such an extent that I talked myself out of the business. But I didn't need a convert to my views on sales recruitment; I did need the business and I lost it.

Why make the same mistake? Always agree with your clients unless it is a subject which definitely affects the business under discussion. You can't agree that a room is suitable for 100 if you know it won't take more than 50; then you have to disagree. If the client has an inflated and unjustified opinion of his own expertise, you are picking your verbal way through a nasty minefield.

What, in fact, do you do with this sort of 'expert'? To contradict him will arouse his anger and to accept his proposals may be impossible. Well, let us take this example of the 'expert' saying that a room can seat a number you know it cannot. You deal with that by agreeing with him!

'Should be just about right, Mr Smith. A hundred for a conference.' You pick up two chairs and go to the front of the room where the first row would be. 'This would be about right for the front row?' Mr Smith agrees. You then put down the two chairs beside each other and start moving them across the room, in turn, to show how many can go in a row. When you reach the other side of the room – leaving space for a gangway – you say, 'Twelve delegates across the room, then?' Mr Smith agrees again. Then you put the two chairs behind each other at the correct distance apart for a row, and move back down the room. When you reach the back wall on the seventh row, you say, 'Seven twelves are 84. Now that's odd. I would have thought we could get 100 in here.' And a slight frown of puzzlement, if you can manage it, does help – and a searching through papers for accurate information. You are still agreeing with Mr Smith, even though you have proved conclusively that he is wrong. Mr Smith can now get back from the limb he has climbed out on without any loss of dignity. Similarly when he states an impossible figure for a budget, you agree that the budget is reasonable, go through the figures and prove that it isn't. The mistake to be avoided like the plague with this type of customer is to give any indication at all that you always knew he was talking nonsense. If Mr Smith gets the impression that you believe you have won an argument, he will punish you by taking the business elsewhere.

We have talked of the 'expert' and the people who are intimidated by the surroundings of your hotel. Let us look at some more types you will meet.

Contrasting with the client suffering from an inferiority complex is the customer who is worried whether your standards are high enough. These clients fall into two groups; a very small number who really do know the business, who have need of high standards and are professional in their approach; and the larger number who are putting on airs – self-styled experts of another kind. For the professional, you have to know your subject very thoroughly. You need to go through the details of the function meticulously, make sound creative suggestions, work closely with the client and behave as an equal expert. In fact, I can remember very few customers who really belonged in that league.

The much larger number of poseurs is a different matter; these people are on ego trips, pretending to expertise they don't possess and drawing for their experience from magazine articles and cocktail party conversation. Even so, they have to be treated with care, for any suggestion that the traditional ceremonies are play-acting will not go down well. The relative merits of the individual wines should be carefully considered – even if they haven't any merit! If you are tasting the wine first, then examine it with care, hold it up to the light, spend time on the bouquet; in fact, put on a show. Remark on the rare experience of dealing with a client who really understands the finer points of banqueting; it may be possible to lay on the syrup too thickly, but I can't actually recall an occasion when a client of this kind didn't lap it all up. Remember, this type of customer is not a real expert. Real experts are invariably diffident and modest about their skill. Therefore you soon recognise the quasi-professional by the 'one-up' remarks which emerge, 'You don't appear to have any 1975 from the north of Alsace', or 'Could I have it garnished with black grapes rather than white?' Don't classify the client on one casual remark. Build up a picture for yourself as the meeting progresses.

Have you ever met the guilt-ridden client? This chap feels indebted to the hotel he has patronised for a long time. The manager of the hotel may not have done anything like as good a job as you can, but he is well liked by the client. The attitude is, 'I can't let old Charlie down'. I feel that way about my garage man, though I could tell you stories about servicing and invoicing which would make your hair stand on end. But I've been going there for years, he's very cheerful and a co-operative fellow, he isn't getting any younger and he knows that I like things done quickly and he is fast. Most important of all, nobody has asked me to switch my custom, but if they did, my inherent and quite misplaced loyalty would make me think twice. To spot this type of customer resistance, the salesman asks, 'Which hotel have you been using for the party before?' Then, having identified the hotel and already knowing the name of the manager – you must know the opposition – you say, 'Oh yes, Charlie Brown'. This is another moment to observe the client carefully. Does he brighten at the name of Charlie Brown, does he frown, shift irritably in his seat or simply look blank? He will normally react to the name and you will then know more about the question of loyalty.

If you establish that he does like Charlie, you then wait until you have completed your sales presentation and tackle the problem in your summing up. You establish that you are providing better value than Charlie, you may well have established the problems that have occurred at Charlie's hotel which you can overcome, and then you deal with Charlie himself. 'It is always a pity, Mr Smith, when you have to make a decision to take your business away from an old friend.' It is, and the thought is going through the client's mind, so you can voice it too. 'The central point though, it seems to me (that's amateur me: if the client argues, we will accept his professional opinion immediately, but we probably *have* got his principal concern) is that you must get that message over to the salesmen/keep within the budget guidelines/ avoid those complaints about the menu', and so on. It is going to come to a choice the client must make, but it will now be an open choice, not one taken behind your back and without your knowledge. You have made the client face a difficult decision, and if you are better – as you should be before you deal with the loyalty to Charlie – the client is finally going to ditch his old supplier.

Another problem is the lazy client, the man who just can't be bothered to make a change. You should be on the look-out for this type when a client arrives late and hasn't had the courtesy to warn you; when he doesn't ring back when he has promised to do so; when he can't be bothered to see the room where the function is to be held, even though he has accepted a luncheon appointment. You look for signs of laziness as you look for other clues to character. If you decide that you could lose the party because of the client's lazy attitude – 'I'll leave it all to Charlie again' – the key task is to build confidence in the client's mind that there will be equally little to do if he gives the business to you. Don't let him raise a finger; get him matches for his pipe rather than have him get them out of his overcoat pocket where he left them. Tell him you will write and confirm because you're sure he has better things to do with his time than write you letters. The idea that he has better things to do with his time – like sitting with his feet up studying the day's racing – will appeal to him.

Give the impression of the eager beaver yourself, hurrying to turn lights on, hurrying to get brochures, banqueting books or a wine list. Let him realise that if he comes to you, there will be masses of energy available to which he does not have to make a contribution. Charlie was not, necessarily, very energetic. It was just that over the years Charlie did it so many times, that now he can do it with one hand behind his back. Your energy doesn't contrast with Charlie's energy; it is a new ingredient to the client, who will be reassured that he can go on being lazy even if he does change hotels.

You have to differentiate between the lazy client and the scared customer. You may feel that 'scared' is a pretty strong word, but there are occasions when a bad function can have a serious effect on a man's career. If the Sales Administration Manager arranges the National Sales Conference badly, if too many things go wrong and the Sales Director or Managing Director feel that the job was bungled, the prospects for the Sales Administration Manager are dim. Many executives are very concerned at this possibility, and the first thing they consider when deciding on a venue is insurance. The insurance they want is an excuse they can trot out to explain their shortcomings, and the best one is that the hotel was at fault but it was the one the company had used many times before. 'How was I to know it would go wrong?' is an excuse which holds water if there was a track record for the hotel having done a good job in the past. You therefore not only have to forward a better product, but produce the insurance as well. This applies not only to the executive who echoes the words of the hit song in *How to Succeed in Business without really*

Trying ('Is there anything you're against?' 'Unemployment'), but to some genuine problems as well. The National Sales Conference really is an important occasion because the sales force probably only gets together once a year and the effect or non-effect of the conference can have marked influence on sales in the coming year. A party for clients which goes badly can have an influence on whether they sell the company's product or not. Particularly where there is competition in entertaining between a number of companies in the same field, the ones which do the job poorly can easily suffer a drop in orders.

How do you provide the insurance? By producing evidence – if you can – of other important functions that his company has held at your hotel. The fact that it was another department or division doesn't matter. Be careful not to attempt to provide the insurance by indicating another company in the same industry which uses you for this type of party. If he happens to dislike the company or believes that it has a poor reputation, then the fact that it chooses you could be a disincentive. I was never wildly impressed when a supplier told me that Magnum Hotels had bought their products. When Magnum went into liquidation I felt justified. Safety products, 'as fitted in the *Titanic*', did not help the sales argument after the ship went down. Another form of insurance for this kind of client is specific detailed confirmations in writing. If things go wrong, the client knows that he can show the letter as proof that the hotel said it understood what needed to be supplied. Finally, if you happen to have worked for a large number of first-class firms in other industries than his own, it is good evidence to place before him.

Many clients come to look at your hotel if you ask them, but they don't buy the product because they are too timid. It isn't the same thing as feeling that they don't belong, because they might be perfectly at home in the surroundings. Their problem is that, being timid, they hate arguing and they simply won't volunteer the information that they are unhappy with your proposals. How do you recognise this problem? The timid client is the man who is always agreeing with you. 'Very nice,' he says and 'Oh, really', and replies endlessly 'Yes' and 'Of course'. The inexperienced salesman may get the impression that everything is going along beautifully, but quite the opposite can be the case. This is the type of client who accepts your recommendation for dishes at lunch, replies to the query of what he would like to drink, with 'What are you having?', and doesn't want you to send back his obviously cold soup or coffee.

What to do? There is a question that establishes whether you are on the right track or not. The question is, 'If you could imagine the perfect hotel, Mr Smith, what do you think it would be like?' If the answer bears no resemblance to the type of hotel you are offering, you know you're in trouble. If the answer is 'They would always serve the food piping hot', you know more about what matters to the client. You also have to encourage criticism. Comments like, 'You know, Mr Smith, none of us buys a really perfect product. There's always a better way of doing things and often the only way we find out is when our clients are kind enough to tell us. For instance, how would you improve *this* hotel, Mr Smith?' You're almost forcing him to criticise, you're helping him to voice his reservations about your product. And you must push him, because otherwise he will leave without voicing them and go somewhere else. How does the timid client ever make up his mind? Very often it is by choosing the safest hotel, the one which everybody uses. So, if that isn't your hotel, you had better get those objections out into the open. Then you have a good chance, because the client finally has been able to speak openly and resolve his fears. As he finds the searching a chore anyway, he should settle for you now that he has got the problems off his chest.

Another type of client you have to watch for is the one with the chip on his shoulder about the hotel industry. That we pay our staff too little or are full of foreigners, are a snooty lot or always vote for the wrong political party. In such company I produce a whole series of character witnesses to speak for me. There is my cockney grandmother, my uncle on the Labour council or my aunt on the Conservative council – whichever is more suitable – my lowly-paid origins or my Uncle with two boxes at Ascot! They may never appear physically but acknowledging their existence is enough. Never argue with the man with a chip on his shoulder against us. The right attitude to adopt when you have finished with your family and friends, is that you quite agree, but he has got to choose one of these dreadful places to hold the function and at least he should support you since you agree with him. The alternative is to tell him precisely where to go and his business will go with him. You must decide for yourself where you draw the line. I do draw it on certain subjects, but this book is about getting banquets. If you want one from this character, don't argue with him.

There is a more unpleasant type of customer even than the unreasonably prejudiced one. There is the man who puts his own greed ahead of his company's interests. He tells you quite openly or in a way that you can't mistake, that he wants his kickback. A bribe by any other name would smell, but there are some countries where it is part of the lack of culture, and you might be asked for one. The right way to deal with the problem is to decide first whether the client is self-employed or an employee. If he runs his own business and wants a few bottles of Scotch put on his company's bill, he is likely to be fiddling the tax man. Hopefully, the tax man will catch him but you can't be responsible for this situation.

If he is an employee, he is fiddling his company. In the latter case, you should tell him that you will have to get permission or agreement and that you will report back to him. You then find out who is his immediate superior and ring him, asking for an appointment. I did this once and I said to the more senior executive.

'I have a problem. I have been doing business with a company for some years and the new man with whom I am dealing is asking me for a bribe. He doesn't mind what I charge his company, but he wants the bribe for himself. What do you suggest I do?'

The executive said to me, 'Very interesting problem. I'll think about it.' I thanked him, left, and got the business the next day after he had fired the man who wanted a bribe. Anybody who tries to steal from the company who employed him should be reported to his own company; otherwise we shall finish up like Banana Republics. The senior executive was very grateful, for goodness knows how much money I saved the company. It is not good sales policy to protect crooks. If you play the game their way and are caught, it is a criminal offence for the man who gives as well as the one who receives.

Nobody can hope to pretend that they are not trying to persuade the client to buy their product. Consequently there is the type of client who distrusts salesmen. Quite possibly he has had some unhappy experience in the past with a hotel salesman, and he is now very suspicious of anybody making a presentation. 'These salesmen will tell you anything . . .' is his credo. If he doesn't put it that bluntly, you can usually judge the type by the way he comments on your statements. He questions them abrasively, trying to trip you up, searching every detail. How do you deal with that? To begin with, you don't show the slightest degree of annoyance. The client should be reassured that you are glad to have a potential customer who obviously knows exactly what he wants and what he is entitled to get. You answer questions thoroughly, and even a bit too thoroughly in the confident expectation that he will get tired of the game if you agree to play it. He wants to know how you avoid cheating him on the pre-dinner cocktails. You insist on producing the control sheets for last night's function. You show him in great detail how he can check that he has only been charged for what he and his guests drank. You ask, 'Have you ever had an occasion when you were overcharged?' He tells you the long saga and you listen intently, and you sadly agree with him all the way down the line. Then you equally solemnly explain how it couldn't happen with you – and it had better be true because this client often knows exactly what he is talking about. Eventually you can reassure him because everybody else will have sworn that he was mistaken and only you will have reassured him that he wasn't.

You can already see how difficult it is to deal with all the clients as if they were cast in the same mould. They are not – and there are still more specific market segments we must examine.

There is the evasive client. You have said everything right, you have answered all his questions, you have not put a foot wrong and still he doesn't buy. Now what's the problem? One possibility is that you have been trying to sell to the man who can't make decisions without consulting his boss. He may have told you that he was the decision-maker, but when it comes to the crunch he isn't. When you run into this kind of blank wall, it is necessary to probe the decision-making process to see if that is the root of the problem. 'Do you have a sort of committee to organise this dinner?,' you ask casually, as if you were learning about the subject as a kind of research project. If the guest mentions that another executive more senior than himself is involved, then the likelihood is that you have the wrong man with you.

How do you tackle this one? It is a serious blunder to deal with the wrong man because you cannot afford to have your sales message diluted by this second-string decision-maker when he eventually tells his boss about the hotel. You need to get to the man in charge and the best way to do it is to discover when your guest is going to be away from the office in the immediate future. 'Do you do a lot of travelling?' 'Where are you off to next?' Establish when the guest will be away and then ring the senior executive on that day. Your excuse to the guest, if he reacts badly in the future, is that you couldn't get him and there was an important fact that you had forgotten to mention. So you spoke to the senior executive in his absence. When you have explained your manufactured point to the senior executive, you can then ask him what he thought of the hotel's proposals and, if necessary, make an appointment to see him in order to sell: this time – to the right man.

Another section of the market is the client with a military background. He is looking for an efficient organisation and he will be more affected than most by prompt action, appearance and a formal businesslike manner. Contrari-wise, of course, the client from one of the more informal industries – show business for example – is likely to be turned off by such an approach. They are normally looking for a more informal relationship, more relaxed, and they usually respond well to an imaginative, creative approach.

You also have to be on the look-out for the pessimistic client. He is the gentleman who won't change because he really doesn't think there's any hope of the event being improved, because he feels that absolutely *nothing* ever can be improved. He is resigned to the same old mediocre standards and your task is to raise his enthusiasm. It is often as easy as raising a sunken liner, but that is the job. Nostalgia is a great help here. You establish an occasion in the past which he remembers with affection because it was a great day for him. Then you isolate what parts of it he remembers best, and try to introduce those factors into the function he is organising this time.

It is one thing to know that clients may not make decisions on the logical grounds of price or quality. It is quite another to spot the problem when facing a client who may be unaware of his own hang-ups or, knowing them, may be intent on concealing them from you. How do you identify what is worrying a client?

It is a major step even to recognise that something might be worrying him. The concept of empathy is not widely used and certainly not as standard practice. You should, as a definite matter of course, consider the likelihood of unconscious problems.

Next you must do your homework. You must learn as much as you can about your client. Does it appear to you strange that the Public Relations Manager in charge of the national conference is a 20-year-old girl? What sort of pressures will that create for her? Is it likely that there is really a senior decision-maker back at the office? Does she appear competent in the questions she is asking? Is she confident or ill at ease? Listen to the comments of the client on other matters; what does he criticise, what does he like? If you can get some background information from another member of the firm, you should do so.

We once had two clients coming from America to fix up a very large conference; one was the Chairman and the other was his travel agent. In such circumstances it is quite usual to set up a bar for the client with the hotel's compliments, a practice which important international decision-makers expect all over the world. So we could have done just that with hardly any effort. Instead we telephoned a contact in the client's company, checked on his preferences and had a bottle of his favourite Jack Daniels bourbon and William & Humberts sherry waiting for him. We also checked on the travel agent, who turned out to be a Mormon, so we took all the alcohol away from his bar. If the business is important to you, leave nothing to chance that can be checked.

You should observe the client very carefully at all times. You can first of all look for signs of nervousness. Only in very extreme cases will you find people twisting their hands or giggling madly, but look for the signs that mean people have not relaxed; are they perched on the edge of seats, or pill rolling? What's pill rolling? It is rubbing your thumb up and down your index finger, a sure sign of nervousness. If the client doesn't like what you are saying, he may avert his eyes, move his chair back a little, cross his arms, or simply drum his fingers in an irritated manner.

Remember the way in which the Americans discovered how women shoppers reacted to the first supermarkets? They set up a camera to film the arrival of the ladies in order specifically to measure the eye-blink rate. Apparently when people are nervous they blink fast, but when they are relaxed the rate drops. So they measured the women's eye-blink rate and found it so slow that the women were obviously almost hypnotised by the enormous selection ahead of them. We may be able to control what we say, but there are any number of other ways by which a keen observer can get some inkling of what we are thinking.

Also be careful to observe the appearance of the client. Do they appear to have put on their best clothes for the occasion, a sign of nervousness, not of respect for your status! The ladies can spot what is fashionable and expensive, though this is often beyond the men. Contrariwise, the men should be able to spot an expensive suit, hand-made shoes, Christian Dior ties. It helps to be able to identify club ties, because people don't wear them by accident. They are, of course, status symbols, but why does the wearer need reassurance? Is it because he considers himself too young for what he is doing? Does he need acceptance because he feels socially inferior? Does the tie represent standards he feels missing in present-day society? To what will you have to adjust in order to avoid hitting a raw nerve? Of course, he might be going to the reunion that evening and so has put on the tie for the one and only time in the year. The task is to be on guard and to observe, so that you can better understand this complete stranger as quickly as possible.

Quite obviously you are still going to make mistakes and rub the client up the wrong way on occasions. But you were going to do that anyway without making an effort to understand the client's personality and thinking processes. The worst that can happen is that you will still upset him, but by endeavouring to understand the clients better, you must have a better chance of avoiding pitfalls. I have not attempted to exhaust all the various types of customer you will meet because there are plenty of books on that subject alone. Just remember that a good product is very often not enough, an amateur attempt at understanding human nature and behaviour helps.

10 Advertising

Advertising in the hotel industry covers the whole range of functions we handle, from small weddings and private parties at one end of the scale to major international conferences at the other – and with a whole host of others in between. I have no idea exactly how much the hotel industry spends annually on banquet advertising of all descriptions. Logically, that money should have been spent wisely, and it must surely run into hundreds of thousands of pounds, if not many millions. Before we discuss how to produce good, and by that I mean effective, advertising, let us first examine whether all the advertising we do *is* justified; whether some of it should be done at all.

I consider that in almost every case advertising is a much poorer means of communication than the alternative means of selling by personal contact. Yet the manager who is not fond of selling, and perhaps has a personal hang-up about it, is inclined to see advertising as an easy way out. It does not involve him in any personal effort in emotional terms; placing an advertisement will not require the injection of energy and confidence that picking up the telephone to call a prospective client does. It enables the manager to spend money himself, rather than trying to persuade a client to do so, which makes a pleasant change. And it reverses the roles of supplier and customer, putting someone else in the position of serving him. All these are good incentives for a non-salesman to opt for advertising! So the first question you must ask yourself, before you spend money on advertising is whether it is really the best way of achieving your aims, or whether it is simply a way of getting out of personal selling. And you **must** answer that honestly.

Certainly advertising can be a terrible waste of money. Few readers notice more than three or four advertisements in a newspaper or periodical they are reading. For one of those to be yours, it has to be more compelling than the full-page advertisements, those in colour, and those produced by the best advertising brains in the country. A very tall order.

Perhaps the most important single point to remember about advertisements is that your customers do not have to read them. If you speak to them, it is difficult for them not to listen, but it is very easy not to read. No matter how important or attractive you think your advertising message is, your prospective clients are under no obligation to give it a second glance. It is no use complaining that people's behaviour is unreasonable, because nobody is in a position to say that they have to be reasonable. It is a hard struggle to get attention for your advertisement, which is why if you advertise at all, every tiny detail must be dealt with correctly.

Also, the results of advertising are often very obscure. Indeed, one way in which many hotels conceal from themselves the lack of results is by ensuring that no-one can tell whether the advertisement worked or not. An advertisement might say, for example, that the hotel has splendid banqueting facilities at reasonable prices. How do you know whether that prompted any bookings? Do you assume that any enquiries in the following weeks are the result of the advertisement? Do you ask everybody who enquires how they came to hear of the hotel? Or do you calmly announce that the space was bought as a 'Prestige Advertisement' – which really means that if it does not work, you have the excuse that it was never bought to do anything so mundane.

Why should this be? The reason is often self-protection. Where there are professional sales managers in hotels today, there has been a considerable increase in the money spent on advertising and often a very sizeable budget is allocated. These budgets, however, can be a sign of 'empire-building'. In some cases, it must be realised that the sales managers may have a vested interest in nobody knowing if the advertising bought with the money was a flop. To have to admit that £10,000 spent on conference advertising did not produce the goods can put the Sales Manager's job in jeopardy, or at the very least produce a big question mark over his technical ability. The advertising agent may not want the results to be accurately monitored, for the same reason. The advertisements were the creation of his employees, and if results were not achieved, maybe another agency could have done better!

When I set out to try to solve the long-outstanding problem of the occupancy of our hotels over the winter weekends, I had been with the company for over ten years, and I still felt that insurance was a wise investment. I recognised that there was a strong possibility that any money spent on Mini Holiday advertising could go down the drain. I therefore put it to the Managing Director that we had always lost a fortune over the weekends in the winter because we couldn't fill the bedrooms. Unless we did something about it, this situation would continue. If we were going to lose £X thousand over those weekends, then the worst that could happen, if we spent £1,000 on advertising, was that we would lose £X thousand + £1,000. If he would agree to our spending that amount, I would guarantee that we would know exactly what happened to the expenditure; i.e. that our advertising would be designed so that we would know the exact results. We went ahead. Guests wishing to come on a Mini Holiday would have to fill in the appropriate application form, and on the basis of how many application forms arrived, we would know exactly how well or badly our advertising had done.

That initial £1,000 expenditure has now grown to over £300,000 a year, but the same rules apply. If something goes wrong with your advertising campaign, the important thing is not to make excuses, but to recognise that it did go wrong. After all, advertising agents or hotel sales managers are not deliberately going to spend the money unwisely. They may make mistakes, but they will be trying. Why penalise them for genuine errors of judgement in one of the most difficult forms of selling known to man?

I offer you eight important rules for successful advertising:

Rule 1 for all advertising (after taking out insurance with the boss!) is that you must provide a means of evaluating the success or failure of the advertisement itself.

Rule 2 is to keep firmly in mind that the advertisement is supposed to appeal to the customers and not necessarily to the Manager, the hotel staff or the Board of Directors. Too much hotel advertising is designed to appeal to the Chairman. The ingredients of such advertising are elegance, distinction, pretty pictures, immaculate staff and an atmosphere of very considerable expense. It is all a lovely ego trip for the company employees to pretend that their banqueting is the equivalent of the setting and standards of Buckingham Palace, but very often it frightens the life out of prospective customers.

The most successful hotel advertising ever is the Stardust promotion of Mini Holidays, which has always featured a printing ink called Dayglo Red. This ink shines with a sort of neon glow and was selected because it was the nearest I could get to a colour that would stop a charging elephant at 200 yards! Not only has it been condemned as vulgar by some senior management, but it has also led to the resignation of eminent advertising agency Creative Directors who refused to be associated with such a loud and unseemly display. It has never won any awards in competitions, but I would not dream of changing it.

The reason is explained in the true story of the railway executive who complained to his local manager that the Mini Holiday posters had been plastered all over the station.

'But we've only put up three,' protested the manager.

'Really?' said the executive, 'but you can see them all over the station.'

'Yes,' said the manager, who realised their strength in a sea of dull posters, 'you can, can't you!'

A poster is displayed to attract attention, not to win awards. All advertising is to obtain business, not to be hung in the Royal Academy. The public saw the posters and bought from the posters. How did we know? Because we asked all the visitors how they learned of the promotion, and 35 per cent said that they first saw it on a poster. Good banquet advertising is advertising that appeals to the largest number of customers.

Rule 3 is that advertisements should state prices. No matter how good the product, the main question all we customers have to ask ourselves is whether we can afford it. That is perhaps one of the more unfortunate facts of life, but it is no less true for being unpalatable.

There has been some improvement in hotel industry advertising since the days when nobody mentioned the tariff – 'Prices on Application' – but still far too much of our advertising omits this most important piece of information. We make the advertising look expensive in its design, and very often in its wording – promising facilities ranging from magnificent to superb – and then leave the reader to guess at the price. If he guesses that it is far above his means – even if we do use expressions like 'great value for money' – we have only ourselves to blame. Advertisements should name prices; if the advertisement is for a conference and you have an all inclusive daily rate of, say £20, then that fact should be communicated in the copy. Why isn't it? Because we have this long tradition that actually to talk about money is lower class! The fact that Rolls Royce mentions price, that estate agents advertise £100,000 houses, and that consortia of banks advertise flotations for millions of pounds, affects our thinking not at all. This is another case, I am afraid, where they are not 'all out of step except my Charlie'. Charlie is out of step, even if he has been doing it that way for a hundred years.

Rule 4. If Rule 3 is to put in the price, then Rule 4 is to assess the cost of the advertising in terms of the additional profits you can make if it is successful.

Let us take as an example an advertisement to sell a New Year's Eve ball; the balance sheet is illustrated (Fig. 8). We will assume to make it simple, that you sell the tickets for £10 apiece. You know that your costs are going to be £7 a head, including the band, cabaret, food, staff and everything else. You also know that you can accommodate a maximum of 200 guests. Your total profit therefore, is a potential £600 assuming that the customer is not going to be asked for more money for drinks, cigars and so on. Obviously, then, you cannot spend more than £600 on advertising the event, without finishing up making a loss. As you can expect some customers, even if you do no advertising, you also have to assess what the number will be – let us say 100. Because your band and cabaret costs are fixed, irrespective of the numbers listening, with 100 guests you might make only £1.50 a guest profit. You are therefore trying to spend money on advertising not to make £600 profit, but to raise the profit from £150 to £600. Therefore, if you spend more than £450, you would have been better off not to advertise at all. Of course you might have other reasons, such as feeling that the room would look empty with only 100 people in it, but we are discussing the financial raison d'être for advertising. There is a further point: spending £450 is going to be sensible only if you do sell out, i.e. if you get the full extra 100 people you need. If you get only an extra 50 guests, you will have spent £450 for an extra £225 profit, so you will lose £225 on the promotion. This is a crucial point to understand, and as you can see from the illustration, this is the way it has to be assessed. Time and again there are advertising campaigns recommended which cannot possibly be profitable even if most of the spare capacity is taken up.

The break-even point, if the whole £450 is spent on advertising, is 166 covers, two-thirds of the spare capacity having been sold, through advertising.

New Year's Eve Ball

Expenditure		*Income*
Food and service	£5.50 a guest	£10 a ticket
Band and Cabaret	£300	

Profit and Loss for 100 guests

Expenditure		*Income*	
Food and service	£550	From sale of 100 tickets	
Band and Cabaret	£300		£1,000
	£850		

Profit £150

Profit and loss for 150 guests, spending £450 on advertising

Expenditure		*Income*	
Food and service	£825	From sale of 150 tickets	
Band and Cabaret	£300		£1,500
Advertising	£450		
	£1,575		

Loss £75

Figure 8.

How to Sell Banquets

As that example shows, it is essential to decide what additional profit an advertisement can provide, and then to set your advertising budget at a point where a reasonable percentage of success will cover your costs. In our example, the point at which the costs are covered is when 166 tickets are sold, which shows an improvement of two-thirds on the estimated numbers you would get without any advertising. This is called the break-even point, and you should aim to reach it when you have sold maybe half of the extra capacity, rather than two-thirds. This depends though on how much success you have had in the past. The greater your record of success in the past, and therefore the likelihood of success, the more you can spend. Thus the amount an impressario will pay a world-famous violinist for a concert may be almost the total profit from a completely sold-out concert hall. As success is assured, this is reasonable. If the artist is less famous, the impressario will offer a smaller fee so that the concert will still be profitable, even without a full house. Remember that when you spend money on advertising, you are spending profit.

Rule 5 concerns what people call the 'spin-off' from advertising.

The argument is often advanced that advertising produces spin-offs; thus you may not sell all your tickets for the New Year's Eve Ball, but the advertising mentioned the name of your hotel, so other people will come during the course of the next week or the next year. There is no proof of this whatsoever and it is a far better discipline to give no weight to such claims. Judge your advertising by the results of your first objective, and do not make the excuse of peripheral advantages which are little more than smoke screens to hide failure.

What, you may ask, about all those hotels who just advertise, 'Stay at the magnificent Splendide-Ritz-Palace'. Or those who emphasise the size of their smile and the warmth of their welcome? Can they all be wrong to put their famous names before the public? Well, unless they can prove the worth of this kind of advertising in terms of hard cash, of extra profits in the bank, then I can see no purpose in the exercise, except to pour the money down the drain.

Rule 6 refers to timing.

Take, for example, the wide range of magazines whose readership might well be interested in booking conferences. Apart from the initial problem of the readers seeing your advertisement at all, the other question is whether they saw it at the right time – when they were thinking of making their decision. If they read it six months before they had to make up their minds, the likelihood of their remembering your proposition is remote. You could, of course, advertise in every issue on the principle that you would then be in time for every decision, but the cost would be very high. The advantage of having a salesman is that, once he has discovered the decision-making timetable, he can contact the client when the right moment comes and not take a chance that, with a monthly magazine, is presumably an 11-1 shot. Those poker players who have tried to turn two pairs into a full house will know that 11-1 is not very attractive if you want good results.

The timing of advertising applies to Christmas programmes, dinner-dances, and every other type of function. You have to decide what the pattern is, and then aim your advertisement to hit your public just before the decision-making time arrives. The right time for holiday advertising is after Christmas; the right time for selling Christmas programmes is usually in September/October, after the summer holidays.

Rule 7 deals with what you are going to say and to whom are you going to say it.

Most advertisements for hotels lack conviction. Every boarding house is supposed to have magnificent facilities in superb surroundings. The language of hotel advertising has become debased over the years. The key to this problem is to decide what the customer wants to know about your product in order to decide to buy it. The prospect of magnificence is probably far too exotic to attract most ordinary people, and it is usually not necessary to say it about the hotels which are genuinely magnificent because the customers will know already. You have to decide to whom you are talking, and what they consider important. We have already discussed what matters to the customer in Chapter 1. We have to draw inferences from what they feel is important.

For example, when advertising conference facilities, I have often seen hotels put over the message, 'Come to the Splendide and you can safely leave all the arrangements with Miss Smith, our Conference Officer'. Now we know that the national sales conference may be the make-or-break day for the company's profits next year, the most important occasion in the Sales Director's calendar. To suggest that a Conference Officer, no matter how attractive, can take this on as if it were a few friends in for coffee, hits a very raw nerve indeed. The client might be impressed if you suggested that your entire Board of Directors was prepared to devote their week solely to his problems, because that would be reflecting his view of the importance to be attached to the event. It might not be credible, but it would at least show that you were on the same wave-length as the customer. You can see that a bad advertising message can be entirely counter-productive; that you might have been more likely to get the business if you had not advertised. Advertising is a two-edged sword.

Deciding what to say is one thing: who to say it to is another. You have to appreciate that you cannot say it to everybody. People want to buy different things and you cannot appeal to every segment of the market. To claim to be both traditional and modern, high quality and low price, informal and formal, distinguished and homely, elegant and welcoming, is not going to carry conviction. By claiming to be all things to all men you are always in danger of being nothing to anybody.

You therefore have to decide which section of the public you want to attract.

How to Sell Banquets

By all means select the largest if you so wish. There are more people interested in a well-cooked steak than in *taramasolata,* but there is normally less competition for the clientèle who like Greek delicacies. Are you going to go for a large or small section of the market? It is a crucial decision. I have always preferred the largest markets myself. Now how do you attract people to read the advertisements?

Rule 8 is always to get a great headline; the simplest example is the classic advertisement for the company selling hearing aids. The headline is 'Deaf?' That immediately stopped almost everybody in the market for the product when it first appeared. The headline said it all. A great deal of hotel advertising fails to achieve that sort of impact. Indeed it could fairly be described as dull and pedestrian, and as a marketing weapon it was hardly used at all even as late as the 1960s. One of the reasons for the lack of imagination in hotel advertising is again the fear that such an advertisement will 'lower the tone'; but hoteliers worry more about the tone than customers do in this increasingly egalitarian society.

There are your eight rules. Now it would be well worth your while to read a book on advertising. A single chapter of mine cannot do more than sketch in the brief outlines of a subject which sustains a major industry of copy-writers, account executives, creative directors, media buyers, film directors, camera men, designers and goodness knows who else. It is indeed the complexity of the industry which prevents many hoteliers from even trying to understand how to create good advertising. They take one look at the mountain of technical knowledge and decide not to bother.

Let us now try to understand the fundamentals of advertising as a base from which you can study the subject in more detail.

Typefaces

The letters making up the words in your advertisement can be of different styles and each style is called a typeface. There are many hundreds of different typefaces, and your problem is to select the one which suits you, though you will, to an extent, be restricted by the variety the printer has in stock. In any case you would be well advised to keep to the well-tried typefaces. Leave it to the professionals to get the best out of fashionable ones; yes, there are fashions in typefaces. Every year or so as new and different designs come on to the market, you suddenly see a number of major companies using that fresh style for their advertising. But, as with ladies' fashions, the style changes again and nothing looks as old-fashioned in advertising as yesterday's typeface. You might not have recognised this yourself, but as you go round the hotel, look at your signs and remember when they were first put up. It is quite possible that they were designed in the typeface fashionable in that year; if so, you will find them looking old-fashioned today. There was, for example, a Victorian copperplate type which was very fashionable in the 1950s; it labels the decor as 25 years old as soon as you see it today, not just to a professional, but subconsciously to a large section of the general public as well.

How can you avoid these fashionable typefaces? Get a book of sample styles from any printer and look through it, rejecting any typefaces that look gimmicky. You want to go for one of the 'classics', such as one called Times, which I consider very good for hotel advertising.

King William

Let us look at a word in Times (above) and dissect it. Notice first that there are small pieces on the sides of the K and more small pieces at the top and bottom of the i. These pieces are called serifs, and one of the major distinctions between typefaces is whether the lettering has serifs or does not in which case it is called **sans serif.** The purpose of the **serif** is to help the eye along the line. In the same way the margins of white space are to help the eye, having finished one line, to pick up the next. If you have a sans serif typeface, the eye tends to be guided up and down rather than across the line and this makes reading more difficult. That is why almost all books are printed with serif typefaces.

Why, then, does anybody ever use a sans serif one? The answer is that in headlines the sans serif typeface stands out more boldly than a serif face. Many of our more dramatic newspapers, like the *Daily Mirror* and *The Sun,* choose that style to make more impact. Because a sans serif typeface shouts that bit more loudly, and because the papers appealing to the more educated readership use serif typefaces, there has come to be a social connotation to the choice of print. Serif typefaces are considered rather upper class and sans serif typefaces rather lower class. Do the public realise this? Not always consciously, by any means, but subconsciously they do, and your advertisement can discourage your potential customer because it does not look attractive to him, even if he could not tell you why. The Times typeface looks elegant, and therefore suits a lot of hotels. If your market is not looking for elegance, then choose a sans serif style.

One of the major mistakes hotel amateurs make in advertisements is to try to cram too much into the available space. To take an extreme example of the other option, I remember one very successful advertisement for the Carlton

How to Sell Banquets

Hotel in Cannes which was placed soon after the restrictions were raised on taking foreign currency abroad. The advertisement occupied a full page, but apart from a small illustration of the Carlton at the bottom and the hotel's name and address underneath, it had only two words on the page: 'Welcome Home'. A great many people commented on the sentiment and remembered it months and even years afterwards. A lot of poster advertising is equally sparse in the number of words used attempting to get over the right message in immediate terms.

What size should the letters in your advertisement be? The measure of type is called **point** size, just like feet or inches. The smallest point size that people can comfortably read is 8 point, and 10 point is better. You can get almost any number of words into a small space if you don't mind your customers having to look for magnifying glasses before they can read the message, but otherwise you are restricted by the size of advertisement you buy. If you write too many words, they will have to be set in type which is too small to read comfortably. Ask your printers how many words he can get into the space, with decent margins and in 10 point type. Remember to leave space for a headline, and that some parts of your message might benefit from being in a larger 'display' size of type.

Printing Processes and Artwork

Artwork is the way your advertisement is arranged, ready for the printing process to begin. There are two printing processes you have to know about; letterpress and litho. The smaller the job, the more likely it is to be done **letterpress.** This is where a piece of paper goes over raised letters like a children's printing press. It gets an impression from the raised letters and none from the sunken part. **Litho** works on the principle that grease and water do not mix. So, if the image – either words or pictures – is made grease receptive and the non-image areas are made water receptive, ink and water can be applied to the receptive areas and an image transferred to paper. In **offset litho,** the image is transferred from an anodised aluminium plate on to a rubber blanket and thence on to paper. Litho is a cheaper process if you are producing a large quantity of material, such as a hotel brochure. Otherwise it is likely that you will use letterpress. In that process the artwork is the design which is copied by the printer. The photographs or drawings are made in metal in what are called **blocks.** The blocks and the type are put together in a metal frame, locked tightly, and your message is ready to print letterpress. Otherwise the artwork is the whole picture to be photographed for the litho plate.

If you are producing an advertisement, it is very expensive indeed to change the artwork at the last minute. It is expensive anyway to produce artwork because it is a highly technical job. The technicians can easily make the alterations, but their time is very costly. Therefore you should try to get your ideas completely clarified at an earlier stage. If you are using a professional designer, the first stage is called a **scamp.** This is just a very rough drawing to give some indication of the basic idea. After that – if you like the idea – you can go to a **dummy** which expands on the concept and gives you a slightly better indication of the finished product. When the dummy is produced, there is also a typed set of the words which are suggested. The wording is called **copy,** as against drawings and photographs. If you don't like the initial copy, it costs nothing to alter a typed sheet of paper and now is the time to do so. After that, having approved the dummy and the copy, you go to artwork. At that stage, the only alterations should be spelling mistakes on the part of the printer or agency, the correction of which is not charged to you.

Colour Printing

Of course any advertisement looks better in colour and the extra cost is more and more accepted. There are now machines which can print all the colours at the same time so that a piece of white paper goes in at one end and comes out as a 4-colour brochure at the other. Let me explain the process of producing colour photographs very simply, because poor photographic reproduction spoils many brochures in our industry.

When you look at a printed photograph, you are looking at a very large number of coloured dots of printing ink. If you look at the photograph through a magnifying glass, you can easily see the dots. The thicker the group of dots, the stronger the colour, and in order to get shades you will see one dot over another. These dots are printed according to a pattern in a metal plate called a **colour separation.** There is a colour separation for each of the three primary colours – red, blue and yellow – from which you can make up the whole rainbow and one for black. Those four plates with the dots on them are printed one on top of the other, and when this has been done, your colour photograph is on the paper. When the photograph looks poor, it is because the colour separations are poor. This can be either because you have a bad printer or because the original photograph was a poor specimen. If it was blurred, the result on your brochure will look blurred. It is very important therefore, to ensure that the material you give the printer is up to standard.

There are fashions in colour just as there are in typefaces, and they are just as ephemeral. Any lady will tell you what colours are fashionable this season, and which were in vogue last year and are therefore very old-fashioned now. If your advertisement is for ladies and is not meant to last for years – our New

Year's Eve Ball again – then the fashionable colours can be used to attract attention. Colours also reflect class consciousness. In general terms, the higher up the social scale you go, the more popular you will find pastel shades, whilst the bright primary colours are more popular with less educated people. That is why you see the detergent manufacturers using primary blues and reds rather than subtler shades. They want to appeal to the largest segment of the market.

One of the major problems in deciding what will look attractive in colour printing is which colours go together. Usually, since banqueting printing is not sufficiently important to justify the intervention of a professional advertising agency creative director, hotel managers have to make their own decisions, and there are many occasions when the final results are poorer than they had hoped. The solution here is to ask for – and if necessary pay for – advice from somebody who is properly qualified. The best yardstick I was ever given was to remember that nature never makes a mistake with colours. If you see the colours together in flowers or in the countryside, you can be sure that they are attractive and compatible.

Paper

Paper comes in all kinds of different qualities and the appearance of your promotional material depends to a great extent on the one you choose. It is also worth pointing out that, on an average print run, about 40 per cent of your printing costs are due to the cost of the paper. Before you order more than you need, remember that element of your costs.

The types of paper available for printing vary from the kind you use for carbon copies of letters to the very highest quality used to produce books on classical art, but we can content ourselves with discussing two types of paper suitable for brochures and promotional material: cartridge and coated art. **Cartridge paper** is dull in appearance and **coated art paper** is very shiny. We use the former for letterheads and the latter for brochures. Both can be used for menu cards, although cartridge paper is more usual. If you are duplicating a menu, it is not advisable to use a coated art paper because the ink absorption is poor unless the printing is professionally done. It is a mistake to skimp and save on the quality of paper. If it is not thick enough, the printing on the back shows through at the front. Furthermore, brochures printed on this paper tend to flop over when put in a brochure rack.

Few things give a better return on investment than a quality product presented on good quality paper. Imagine the sort of note paper you would expect to get from the Chairman of a large multi-national company. It is, of course, possible that, being the Chairman of such a high-powered organisation, he doesn't bother with very high quality paper because his title is enough; but we do tend to equate high quality paper with a high quality product.

One problem to remember is that when coated art paper is folded a crack usually develops in the surface. It is only a superficial crack, but as the printing is done on the surface, it gives the appearance of a white line through the message or illustration. Therefore, if you can avoid printing on the fold, you will get a more attractive visual result.

The printer must be relied upon to recreate the colour tint you want when you supply a sample of the colour. This is because the shade of the colour is affected by the type of paper on which it is printed. As I write I am looking at one ink printed on nine different types of paper and the results vary from Cambridge Blue to Oxford Blue. So give the printer an example of the colour you want, and leave him to decide which ink to use to give you the proper result.

Copy Writing

The words you put in an advertisement are there to sell a product to an individual. A lot of hotel advertising forgets the individual. It simply announces the product without trying to appeal to the client. So it might announce, 'Splendide Hotel, Excellent Conference Facilities, Superb Cuisine, Ample Garaging, Remarkable Value for Money, Perfect Acoustics'. All very attractive as a catalogue of the hotel's virtues, but the advertising message still doesn't talk to the individual reader. All good journalists write as if they were talking to just one person, the kind of reader they imagine is attracted to the paper. As I write this book, I visualise you as a reader and try to imagine what you want to read and how you want it presented. So it is with good advertising.

What might the King William Hotel have said about its conference facilities if they were exactly the same as those of the Splendide? First we'll need a headline: how about 'Not Another Conference!' People who organise them find them a lot of work and capable of producing every kind of problem. The headline reflects one response to the idea of conferences, but it also contrasts nicely with the other advertisements which will be saying that conferences should be held at their hotels. Our headline appears to say the opposite and therefore will stand out. But read on: 'Well, it's a hard slog isn't it? You've got to get them all there on time, teach them, inspire them, feed them, entertain them, put them up and raise the ésprit de corps as much as possible. That's a pretty big order, but the King William is a pretty big hotel. And we can help. You've got ample garaging for the cars, seven conference rooms of different sizes to choose from, and a brigade of chefs who have been complimented by everybody from Unilever to the local architects' A.G.M. There are 75 bed-rooms, you've got peace and quiet for the meetings and a convivial atmos-phere when the day's work is over. And you'll find that we do know that every detail is important, and that budgets and timetables are made to be rigidly applied. We can quote the high opinions of some very good customers. Can we please quote you?'

What we are trying to achieve – and only the results will tell us if we have been successful – is a message that conveys an understanding of the problems the organiser faces, and a readiness to help solve them. Notice a number of points:

1. It doesn't matter if you use slang occasionally, no matter what your old English master told you. 'A hard slog' succinctly sums up how most confer-ence organisers think of the days of the meeting; they will be glad that at least one hotelier recognises it.

2. You have acknowledged the importance of factors they too consider vital: the garaging, quiet rooms, ésprit de corps, and so on. But you have also picked out the two vital ones of timetable and budget. They want to know that you appreciate their priorities.

3. Every so often the words should be clever enough to make it seem worthwhile reading on. The contrast of 'pretty big order' with 'pretty big hotel'. We have switched meanings on 'pretty' and it wakes the reader up, makes him more interested in what might come next. Similarly with 'quote the high opinions' and 'can we please quote you?' We have switched the meaning of 'quote'. Good copy should be interesting copy.

4. Don't be afraid to back up your claim with the recommendation of your satisfied customers. Ask their permission, first, of course, but if they are satisfied there is no reason why they should be unhappy to be associated with your advertisement.

It is not possible to generalise about the tone of your copy, whether it should be frivolous, dignified, elegant or simple. Every hotel appeals to its own market and must decide for itself what that market is like. But it is important to select what the market wants and not what the hotel thinks it ought to want. Copy which is written to make the hotel management feel important is useless.

We can try to make a few mild generalisations on that understanding. Basically, the hotel industry is in show business. Whether we are looking after businessmen, holidaymakers or tourists, we are more often than not part of their leisure activity. When people are off duty they do not want to feel it is necessary to be dignified. Copy should therefore take into account the need to convey a holiday mood. Only when dealing with the technical side of hotels –

146

running conferences, cooking and serving food, attention to detail – should the copy remain serious. Our audience is not likely to be literary, sometimes not even literate. The words we use should be simple enough to convey the message simply. The sentences should be either short or split up with careful punctuation, and the sentences should have a degree of creative imagination.

Advertising within the Hotel

It is all too easy for a client to miss your advertisement in a newspaper or magazine. It is much more difficult for him to miss it inside the hotel. As he stands waiting for the lift, travels up in the lift, comes in for lunch from his nearby business, or reaches his bedroom, almost any decent advertisement you place before him is going to attract his attention, and reading it will help pass the time. We have a captive audience for our advertisements in the hotels, but all too often we waste the opportunity to sell to them effectively. We simply are not professional enough in the way we produce the advertisement. What it comes down to is a series of 'don'ts'.

1. Don't make the advertisement too small. The display in the lift or lobby must look impressive. Usually they are so small you have to put on your glasses to read them. Remember a lot of people have to wear glasses to read and won't bother to put them on to look at display advertisements. Think of the size of the *table d'hôte* menu advertised in lifts; it seldom looks worth reading or worth the money being charged. We are talking about display advertising, so display it in the grand manner.

Advertisements are usually too small because hotels are schizophrenic on the subject; they want to get people to come for the dinner-dance but they don't want to lower the tone by actually advertising it! They equate small with discreet, rather than with insignificant, which is quite a different matter.

2. Don't penny-pinch on the production. I have seen advertisements in luxury hotels for dinner-dances where a 10 by 8 inch black-and-white photograph of the band was supported by nothing more than a handwritten invitation to attend. The appearance would have been discouraging on the noticeboard of the local Y.M.C.A., let alone a luxury hotel. Find yourself a decent professional in the town who is prepared to do some freelance work for you, and produce good-quality advertisements with impact.

3. Try to create a house style. Don't have all the advertisements in different colours with different typefaces, all sizes and shapes. The house style can stem from the fact that you use the same colour combinations, the same typeface or the same designer with his own particular style of drawing. Don't give the impression that every time you produce an advertisement, you start from scratch. Even if you do only a little advertising, you should be just as anxious to create a brand awareness as Marks and Spencer or Smirnoff Vodka.

4. Have your display advertisements framed properly. Don't fall down at the last hurdle with scruffy presentation. If you look at menus in hotel lifts, the *table d'hôte* has so often been put in crooked, presumably by a junior member of the staff. Much as I admire the inventors of self-adhesive tape, it was not designed to create permanent displays; it tends to discolour over a long period of time and always looks like a temporary expedient. Displays should be mounted so that they appear to be permanent, and that really means a first-class glue. Keep the glass and frame clean so that it never looks grubby.

I am quite sure that a lot of internal advertising fails to convince because it is just too tatty. It is not the product which is bad value for money; it is the presentation which makes it look that way.

If you want to see good internal advertising, walk into any Hilton. Their efforts are always professional, always attractive, always prominent and invariably spotless. Most hotels may not have Hilton's budget for internal advertising, but we can all aim for the same level of technical accomplishment.

Classified Advertising

Hotels have been using classified advertising for many years, and Christmas programmes, holiday offers and special events have all been sold through this type of presentation. Of course, it has only very limited relevance for banqueting, largely because nobody reads classified advertising to find out where to

Figure 9. The use of a small classified advertisement that can attract interest.

WE'RE ALL ON YOUR SIDE

If you're happy at the King William you'll tell your friends and come again yourself. That's why we're still in business.
King William Hotel
Tel: Barchester
 (0998) 121 5661
Banqueting for up to 300.
Certainly you can afford it.

THE KING WILLIAM

hold a banquet. But even for other forms of hotel advertising I think it is inferior to the American use of small space as compared with an example of how this might look if a British hotel tried the same technique (Fig. 9).

If you are going to use classified advertising, try to be different from your competition. The most successful use of classified advertising was by a London estate agent (called Roy Brooks) whose copy – for houses the vast majority of his readers had no intention of buying – was a 'must' for anybody reading *The Observer* on Sundays. Can you imagine deliberately turning to a classified advertisement because you enjoy the humour and style of the writer? In our own industry, the indefatigable Joe Barnett of Barnett's Smoked Salmon also has a large following for his copy-writing, even from those who are not in the market for his products. In both of these cases it is the personality which comes through the copy, the humour and off-beat approach which fascinates.

To sum up, then, advertising is a terribly difficult marketing weapon to use properly. It demands great skill and it is very expensive. Most hotels would be well advised to steer clear of it in the banqueting and conference field, and to use the money they were prepared to set aside for the purpose to hire a permanent salesman to do the job.

11

Public Relations

Of all the types of marketing in the hotel industry, public relations is probably the best known because of the immense success of the Savoy Company in keeping its name before the public. We all take off our hotelier's hats to the Savoy for their enterprise, but for some reason most hotels think that the art of public relations is only applicable to the great luxury hotels. The idea that it could equally well be exploited for their own property does not seem to cross their minds. Indeed, most hoteliers only visualise publicity of one kind, and that is bad publicity. They live in some trepidation, if not actual fear, of the unforeseen disaster which is going to have the press swarming round the lobby like bees – or rather vultures – to pick over the bones of the hotel's suddenly expired reputation. As they see it, the press is more likely to be the enemy in the bushes, rather than the friend in need.

This attitude comes from a lack of understanding of the problems of the press. The press is an industry where the expensive cost is manpower. The advertising pages are very lucrative, but the editorial costs a fortune to produce. Salaries, expenses, the cost of provincial and overseas offices are all very high indeed. Anybody, therefore, who can reduce these costs is very welcome and someone who supplies a good news story comes into that category. The Savoy provides good news stories and it provides them for the national press, though most of us cannot aspire to that. The local press is easier to satisfy; and in banqueting, their readers are very important because a lot of our business comes from local sources. If we provide newsworthy stories, the local press will almost invariably print them, and the hotel will get the benefit of having its name mentioned in the editorial columns. Obviously both sides should be very happy with the arrangement, but hotels miss the opportunity time and again. We all have events taking place at the hotel which are newsworthy, yet we fail to send out the news.

How to Sell Banquets

Now other industries do not fail. There are press releases coming from all over the place: from government departments; from manufacturers as diverse as motor cars, cosmetics and cat food; from the armed forces; the entertainment world; and from political parties. A lot of it is frantically dull. By comparison, hotels have glamour and human interest. People enjoy reading about the functions, the celebrities, the high society life; but as we don't produce the stories, the papers cannot print them, and they are left with no alternative but to tell us about some new fertiliser being produced or the future shape of the steel industry. If you saw how much of the editorial section of newspapers was filled with press releases, rather than the efforts of hard-working journalists, you might well be very surprised.

What we must do, therefore, is to identify what banqueting stories are going to be of interest to the press, and then to present them so that the hotel's name figures in the write-up.

What stories do we have that will interest the press? To begin with we have weddings, and pictures of happiness make a nice change from rail crashes or wars. You very often see wedding photographs in local newspapers; but invariably it is the local photographer who has taken a group in front of the church. It could just as easily be the bride and groom waiting to receive their guests at your hotel, but either that picture is not taken, or it is not sent to the paper.

Then we have the important guests of honour who give speeches after dinner. Their offices will usually be glad to supply a press release of what they said. If the speaker comes from another district, you can send a photograph and press release to the local paper in that town, too. Do not forget the trade magazines. When a new product is launched in your hotel, send a photograph and details to the trade paper; when an officer of an association speaks; when an annual dinner is held; there are endless opportunities.

There are charity balls, retirement dinners, foreign visitors and exhibitions – these all have an appeal to local newspaper readers. Indeed, there can be very few events taking place at your hotel which will not interest some readers somewhere. You have sporting events for the sports editor, events of interest to the women's page editor – a fashion show or cookery demonstration, perhaps – and to the entertainment page.

So why doesn't it happen? I think that a number of hoteliers consider that while their costs in terms of photographs and management time are easily identified, the benefit of going to the trouble is less clear. They worry whether the paper will use the material but forget to mention the source of information – the hotel. That very seldom happens; almost all newspapers and trade magazines play scrupulously fair and if they use a press release, they mention the name of the product.

Another argument advanced for neglecting public relations is that the public pay little attention to what they read in the papers, and that seeing the name of the hotel mentioned makes no impression on them. It is surely difficult to accept that argument if, at the same time, money is spent on advertising the name of the hotel, and if it is accepted that much of our business should come from personal recommendation. The fact that the event is being held in your hotel is a personal recommendation from the organisation concerned, and a newspaper is the best way of spreading the message as widely as possible.

The main cause for the seeming indifference to PR is a lack of knowledge of how to go about getting the free publicity. Strangely enough, it is one of the simpler skills to master. A good press release should ideally have the following attributes:

1. A Photograph: The photograph of a speaker of some distinction at the rostrum will do a power of good for the hotel if the front of the rostrum has the hotel's name in large, clear type. The photograph then conveys to the reader that distinguished guests use your hotel. If it is a wedding group, try to ensure that the manager is hovering in the background or at one side looking helpful and benevolent. He will be identified in the caption to the photograph. If the group only consists of the bride, the groom and the manager, so much the better.

2. An 'Angle': Not a geometric one, but some special aspect of the event which can make the news story that little bit more interesting. This isn't always easy, by any means. If the paper prints photographs of weddings every week, getting some new angle is almost impossible. That is why a wedding photograph in the hotel will get printed on its own merits; it makes a change from the church porch. Photographs of army weddings with officers crossing swords for a path of honour is an extreme example of an 'angle' which will always get printed, but a hotel cannot hope to be quite so lavish. You have to try to use a special wedding cake, a bouquet in a particular shape, the juxtaposition of the young couple with a centenarian guest or some other element which is unusual.

If a manufacturing company is launching a new product, the paper will print a picture of something unusual, such as the product reproduced in chestnut purée, ice or ice-cream, or as a cake. The extra publicity will also please your commercial client, as we saw in the chapter on creative banqueting.

The 'angle' also applies to the wording of the press release. It is no accident that ministers choose public meetings to make outrageous remarks. The remarks are designed to get publicity, not necessarily to be government policy. When one political party is engaged in its annual conference with the eyes of the press upon it, the other parties try desperately to think up some angle which will divert attention on to them during the crucial week. If you see one of them about to take his first parachute jump, do not wonder why; because publicity is the answer. In the case of a hotel, you are also looking for the phrase in the speeches which will make good editorial. It can be a joke, a fierce defence or a fierce attack; but something that people will read.

3. A Quotation: If you cannot find anything particularly newsworthy to put into the press release, try to include a quotation of some kind. If the banquet is a private event, be sure to get the permission of the speaker for the inclusion of the wording; remember the fate of the gentleman from British Leyland who was quoted without his knowledge and had to resign. Indeed the press release should always be cleared with the organiser of the function, whether Sales Director or mother of the bride, to ensure that you are not upsetting the apple cart. It is only on very rare occasions, however, that your efforts will meet with any opposition. More often than not, the client will be delighted that the hotel is trying to publicise the event.

4. Correct Wording: A press release should deal only in facts and not in opinions. Describe the bride's dress; but don't say she looked beautiful in it. That is the part the journalist will add, even if he doesn't know! By all means state that the guest of honour was 6 ft 3 in and wearing full evening dress; but don't say he looked distinguished, because that too, is the journalist's job. Just state the facts.

Remember the Chairman's dinner that Mr Coxwell was arranging some chapters ago? How will the press release appear when we send it out the day after the event? The photograph is easy enough; the Chairman is standing at the rostrum, and the hotel's name can be seen clearly. The wording might be as follows:

> The Chairman's dinner of Canwe, Seldom & Co Ltd. was held at the King William Hotel last night (March 21st) in the Hastings Room. One hundred and fifty senior executives of the company were present to hear the Chairman, Owen Seldom, outline the future policy of the company. This will include the employment of a further 150 staff in the next twelve months. After a dinner prepared by Chef Antonio Cardinelli, which featured *Piccata de Veau au Marsala* as the main course, Mr Seldom said,
>
> 'We have a responsibility to provide work for the unemployed in our city, and we hope to play our full part in achieving that worthy objective.'

That, incidentally, is our objective too, because in the hotel we have a responsibility to ensure continuous working and higher wages; these are both much easier to provide if we sell more of the product.

Figure 10. Press release for the Chairman's dinner. ▶

The King William Hotel
Cathedral Square, Barchester S4U 3WS
Telephone: (0998) 121 5661 Telex: 123456 Cables: DOMESDAY

PRESS RELEASE

150 NEW JOBS PROMISED AT CANWE, SELDOM DINNER

The Chairman's dinner of Canwe, Seldom & Co Ltd was held at
the King William Hotel last night (March 21st) in the
Hastings Room.

150 senior executives of the company were present to hear the
Chairman, Owen Seldom, outline the future policy of the
company. This will include the employment of a further 150
staff in the next twelve months.

After a dinner prepared by Chef Antonio Cardinelli, which
featured Piccata de Veau au Marsala as the main course, Mr
Seldom said, 'We have a responsibility to provide work for
the unemployed in our city, and we hope to play our full part
in achieving that worthy objective.'

March 22nd 1979

For further information contact Paul Reynolds, King William
Hotel, Barchester. Telephone: (0998) 121 5661.

How to Sell Banquets

A press release like that obviously has to go out after the event unless you are working closely together with the company and have advance information on what the Chairman is going to say. But send it off straight away, so that it reaches your local newspaper in time to be topical – not a couple of weeks later! Check the press date of the paper and then ensure that the copy is with the editor in good time. If the individual in the news story is prominent enough, the newspaper might like to interview him, which would result in a useful 'mention' for the hotel 'I met Sir Hector in the elegant lounge of the King William Hotel . . .' Now you have two personal recommendations; Sir Hector's by staying with you and the journalist who described the lounge as 'elegant'.

The press release should always be written in clear, simple English. It should be absolutely accurate and precise. You need a headline, too, which should, ideally, be short and catchy. '150 new jobs promised at Canwe, Seldom dinner!' would be about right for our own release. And don't forget to put at the bottom of the release the name and telephone number of somebody to contact if the press want more information.

Press releases are typed double spaced on only one side the paper (Fig. 10), with at least 1 inch margins at both ends of the lines. There should be short paragraphs, and the page should always finish at the end of a paragraph, so that if there is a second page it starts with a new one. And don't forget to add the date.

The Savoy and other top-class hotels still send the press lists of important guests who are arriving in the future, so that the papers can plan well ahead to see them. There is no reason why you shouldn't do the same, so go through your banqueting book and see who is coming. Perhaps you have a dinner for the branch office of a building society. The likelihood is that a guest of honour will emerge from Head Office on the night to give a 'State of the Nation' speech. That is your news story, if you get the information from the organiser and his permission to arrange the publicity. Very often the organiser will not know how to do the PR exercise himself, and will welcome your assistance. If the final result is a photograph in the paper of the Branch Manager with his distinguished guest, you are likely to have a client who is particularly grateful to you.

We have talked so far about the public relations possibilities which exist through guests already coming to the hotel. There is another very important field, and that is the public relations stories you invent for yourself. When we have a banqueting room, we do our best to get organisers to book it for functions. If they fail to do so, we have empty rooms, but, of course, we know some weeks in advance that the rooms are going to be empty. If you haven't got a dinner in the main ballroom for a Saturday night four weeks hence, you don't have much chance of a last-minute booking of that size. If you haven't sold it for the second Monday night in January for the last five years, the likelihood of a customer coming in for that evening must be considered remote. So you know that a certain number of days are going to be blank, and you know that differing periods of time in advance. The possibility exists, therefore, for you to change the situation by producing your own banquet and, of course, the obvious example is the New Year's Eve Ball. But what other events can you produce and how do you go about it?

You can do a lot of good for both the hotel and a local charity by creating your own charity ball to raise funds. You obviously need the support of the charity committee, but what organiser would not be delighted? You would offer the food and drink at cost price instead of making the normal profit. The difference between the cost of the event to the charity and the amount they can charge for the tickets would make a sizeable contribution to the cause, and the hotel benefits from a great deal of favourable publicity. Once the guests are in the hotel, they also contribute to the charity through a raffle or tombola, and they contribute to the hotel by spreading the good word and remembering it for their own functions. Since the night you are offering is one when you would not normally have a function, the hotel does very well. The ideal date for such an event is a Friday or Saturday in January.

Then there are the special interest events. There has been a continuous increase over the years in the number of clubs devoted to specific interests, and a hotel can cash in on this popularity by arranging its own event to appeal particularly to such an organisation. One such event is the Speaker's Dinner, where the hotel invites an authority on the subject in which the club is interested to give a lecture. If the club is involved with a sport, for example, then an expert will be able to give tips on play, training methods and the finer points of the game. Such events can be promoted with the sports editor of the local paper. Why should he give such an event his support? Because he, too, is looking for interesting local news stories and you are providing one. In certain cases you can get the paper actually to sponsor such an event – not with money but with the pull that their name and publicity provides. Your part would be to take the financial risk of paying for the speaker and you would undertake not to charge the paper for a specific minimum number of guests; so if nobody bought the tickets, the paper wouldn't suffer financially at all. On the other hand, your losses would really be confined to the cost of the speaker, which need not be overwhelming. The variety of organisations in existence enables you to arrange speaker's dinners for an almost indefinite number of interests, and can be an excellent way of solving that nasty problem of what to do about Sunday nights when there is normally no function business at all.

Remember the importance of the Women's Page Editor. Many ladies are interested in slimming, beauty care, paediatrics and similar subjects which could produce well-supported Speaker's Lunches. Speakers from commercial firms – such as cosmetic houses – will often come for little more than their expenses: they value the publicity, too.

Keeping your name in front of the public is an on-going effort which demands a place in the week's timetable. The results, in terms of publicity, can only be extremely valuable and each week you should decide what additional material you can give the press. To achieve the best results, get to know your local journalists; preferably by inviting them to the hotel and discussing their interests over lunch or dinner. Find out what stories would be useful to them besides the ones we have already discussed. Does the journalist who does the cookery column want some recipes from the chef? Would she like some tips on how to use new seasons' food in different ways? It's all good publicity. Would some of the readers like to take part in a cookery competition where the chef could judge the results?

I don't really recommend the special weeks much beloved of hotels. They don't get a great deal of publicity because they are not novel, and they cost a great deal of money in special preparations and management time.

Hotels are glamorous to the reading public. The hotels that important people use are the ones many of the readers would like to use as well. Publicity is usually as near free as makes very little difference, so take advantage of the possibilities at all times.

12
What it Takes

It seems as if people are often left to make up their own minds how best to deal with customers. For example, have you ever telephoned one of those super-efficient secretaries who snaps out answers at you like a machine-gun? The ice in her voice would freeze drinks through a long summer's afternoon; and yet I don't believe that most of those ladies want to give the impression they do. The trouble is that they equate a cold, clinical approach with efficiency, thoroughness and many other virtues. Nobody has actually told them that they are not coming over well; that their interrogation is giving offence. When I am buying, as against selling, I do not mind somebody asking me my name, but when they ask me my organisation, I bridle. How much longer am I going to be kept waiting to buy the goods I want? So I always announce to the questioner that I am from the East Worthing Communist Party. Ask a stupid question and you will get a stupid answer. Moreover, I start off being irritated with the salesman's manner, which is very bad for the salesman because his main objective is always to be likeable.

I must tell you a true story about naming organisations on the telephone. It so happened that at one of the hotels, the Manager's direct-line number was very similar to that of a local restaurant. He was often disturbed – as we all are – by wrong numbers, and as he didn't give the direct-line number to anybody, when it rang he always knew it couldn't be for him. So he was wont to pick up the telephone and say the first thing that came into his head. One day a potential customer for the restaurant dialled wrongly, the direct line rang, the manager picked up the telephone and said, 'Kensington Mortuary'. 'Good grief,' said the restaurant's potential customer, 'and I wanted to book a table!'

To obtain the maximum amount of business for the hotel, it is not sufficient for the clients to like its amenities; they must also like the people they are going to work with, and initially that means the person who is selling the hotel to them. The great secret of the first-class salesman is that he is liked by such a wide variety of people. You can achieve this only by a clear realisation that to be liked, you have to be likeable. Now the vast majority of people think that they, personally, are thoroughly likeable. Ask the type of manager who is condescending to clients, dictatorial or pompous to his staff, and he will still believe he is likeable. It goes without saying that you are likeable, too, so why imagine that anybody thinks differently about themselves? Yet, in spite of this unanimous agreement on how likeable we all are, there are still any number of complaints about rudeness, poor service, casual attention, haughtiness, superior attitudes and downright bad manners. Something is wrong somewhere, and all the suggestions we shall now discuss on appearance, personality and habits are part of the groundwork on which a likeable individual is going to be built.

Which do you need more – a good salesman or a good product? A good salesman can sell a bad product: he can only sell it once because the client is not going to be satisfied, but he *can* sell it once. Salesmen are paid to sell the product so that they are chary of complaining about it. But every manager should encourage criticism from his own sales staff about the hotel's shortcomings if these are making the hotel difficult to sell. Uncomfortable banqueting chairs, halitosis or B.O., poor amplification and lighting – pretending it does not exist is not going to fool the clients. I once had great difficulty in selling a banqueting room because of the bad lighting. The management at the time would not listen to me, probably taking the fashionable view that salesmen are never supposed to be satisfied with the quality of the product. The problem was genuinely there, though, and eventually I agreed with a particularly good client that he would write to me and threaten to take his business elsewhere if the lighting was not improved. Only then was anything done about it. Afterwards, in total, we did a great deal more business. The banqueting department needs the right equipment to sell most effectively. Nevertheless, a bad salesman cannot even sell a good product, and it costs less to produce good salesmen than perfect products.

To be considered likeable by as many people as possible, the salesman must be able to blend into the client's background. This is fundamental; whether the client is an Eton and Balliol managing director: a bluff, hard drinking, self-made man; or an 18-year-old copy-typist. He or she must feel that the person they meet is a friend, of their kind, one of them. I have a colleague who, in fact, was at Harrow, and he tells the story of the occasion when he was trying to persuade miners in South Wales to use a hotel. He was chatting to the organiser who produced a packet of Woodbines and offered him one. My Harrow friend recalls with professional horror that his immediate reaction was to pull out his gold packet of Benson & Hedges king-size filters and say that he preferred to smoke his own, but he caught himself in time and accepted the Woodbine. The alternative action would have branded him snobbish and superior. Contrariwise – and this illustrates the importance of having the right sales tools – I was once lunching a very successful book-maker and offered him a cigar which he accepted, until he saw that we could only run to Coronas. He gently declined the offer and pulled out a cigar case capable of taking 7-inch Churchills. At that point, we did not look like a quality product.

To blend adequately, the salesman must cultivate an appearance, a varie-gated personality and a fund of knowledge which at first acquaintance enables him to fit in with any group or class. He then has to decide the character of his client and assume a similar character, like a chameleon blend-ing into the scenery. This can be achieved by following certain basic rules.

Right at the beginning you must accept that all men are equal. If you feel inferior, you will find it difficult not to act like an inferior. While respect and courtesy are due to every client, whether Lord or very Commoner, the good salesman never feels overawed, and never attempts to overawe. This is not an easy state of mind to achieve. Much of the rudeness found in hotels stems from the fact that the staff, whether manager or waiter, feel a little uncomfortable with the guest, and often respond by trying to appear superior. Yet the good salesman will tell you that people are seldom rude, thoughtless or unpleasant and that such armour for one's ego is invariably unnecessary. A salesman who needs to feed his ego at the client's expense is definitely in the wrong business.

Appearance is very important. Whether in uniform, like a wine waiter, or in mufti, like a banqueting secretary, everybody can be smart. This is welcomed by most people and antagonises nobody. By smart I mean that shoes should be polished, hair neatly in place, hygienically beyond reproach, a clean shirt, the tie firmly against the collar and neither crooked nor loose. This is elementary to many people, but it is lacking in many more. The Manager can insist on a good personal appearance but many apparently do not.

The appearance of the Banqueting Manager himself raises controversy. Tradition often demands that he wears morning clothes with pin-stripe trous-ers or evening dress at night. For a salesman, this is most unfortunate. The clothes immediately suggest a certain status and attitude which may be anathema to the client you are trying to persuade to use the hotel. An 18-year-old copy-typist on the staff dance committee may be scared stiff of a man who at first sight appears like an Ambassador. The Trade Unionist organising a fraternal gathering may regard you as the epitomy of capitalism, and the bright young thing with the charity dance may just sum you up as not being with it. In common with some of the finest selling companies in the world, I used to favour a dark suit, a plain tie, dark shoes and a white shirt. Today there is a definite leaning to more informal dress even than that; but if you do not know your client well, it is still the safest style. So many people feel that they can sum up a person the first time they see them, that it is essential not to get off on the wrong foot. Of course, a good salesman does not fall into the same trap of believing that an accurate assessment of a client's character is possible at first sight. People are not, in general, that shallow.

Changing your appearance is important; one style, one image is not enough. I have known sales managers who would keep four different types of hat in the car and use the one which fitted in best with the client they were calling upon. One of my colleagues will never wear a suit when selling to Americans, because it immediately establishes that he is different from them. The British pay particular significance to ties to establish a rapport, and so it goes on.

But can you genuinely be different types of people for different clients? The truth is that basically we are all a number of different people; at a funeral we are different from at a football match; within the family circle we are different from a meeting with the Chairman; with a girl friend we are different from with a grandmother. We are the same person with different images. As we have seen, with clients you simply draw on the appropriate behaviour pattern. It takes hard work; with each client you have to bring out all the interest you ever had in the type of background to which be belongs. Unless you have a genuine interest in your client as a person, you can never achieve a rapport. If you actively dislike him, it is much better to pass him on to somebody else rather than to persevere. Everybody has blind spots; I dislike freeloaders and intolerance. On the other hand, I am little affected by a client's bad manners or bullying ways. If you cannot get on with certain types of people, let a colleague try instead.

I am not suggesting that you will do no business with a company without personal friendship, but your time is limited. You have to build up the largest possible clientèle, and you cannot do this if you constantly have to battle to get business from people who remain distant strangers. I have had clients who have been told by their superiors to use other banqueting rooms, and they have gone out of their way to persuade their superiors to change their minds. They did this because they really felt that their staff or friends were safer in the hands of people they knew and liked. Such an attitude saves you a tremendous amount of work. Not only does it do your job for you, but often it brings parties to the hotel which you could never have reached without that personal recommendation.

It must also be remembered that all too often you lose clients because, after some bad experience, they simply move their business to another hotel rather than complain. This does not happen with friends; they complain and they expect things to improve, but they won't leave you unless you let them down on a number of occasions. Criticism is good for the hotel; if the client just leaves, you not only lose his business, but the fault will still be there to lose you more clients. Acquaintances will not help you in this way but friends will.

There are plenty of people who condemn this type of approach to a client as insincere and hypocritical, but clients are seldom stupid. It is only if your interest in them and their problems is quite genuine that they will become your friends. No service to his client is too much trouble to a good salesman, any more than a favour for a friend would be. The client pays the salaries and keeps the business in being, which makes him very likeable, like a generous uncle. Admittedly you have to like people yourself; all sorts of people, old and young, intelligent and stupid, black and brown, men and women. If you don't like them, they won't like you; because over a period you will be unable to disguise your dislike, and without liking them you will find it very difficult to take a sincere interest in them. But then the person who dislikes more than a very few types of people also has no right to be in the hotel business.

While you have to be understanding, helpful, courteous and friendly, you must also remember and accept that the client is entitled to have every fault imaginable. Clients will be thoughtless on occasions, they will be careless, impatient, boastful, garrulous, unpunctual, snobbish, boring, unreasonable, vulgar and probably many other things you dislike as well. You, however, are by no means perfect yourself, and it is not your job to judge your clients. There will be opportunities handed to you at frequent intervals when you can, with perfect justification, rebuke your client, impose penalties and make difficulties. Swallow the rebukes, cancel the penalties and restrain yourself. This client has business you need; that and *that alone* matters.

People will say that you have to draw the line somewhere, and they are right. The line is drawn on the spot where the trouble involved is greater than the profit gained. With a good client, the line lies a very long way from the start of the trouble. If he gives you the business, he is entitled to his eccentricities.

Undoubtedly the difference between a great salesman and an ordinary one is the determination to succeed. A salesman's finest weapon is persistence, and this is perhaps the most difficult thing to cultivate. It is an absolute refusal to admit defeat where there is a victory to achieve. In banqueting, there is often no senior man to encourage and advise on sales problems. You are on your own to succeed or fail without real supervision in the sales area. In other industries there are patterns of sales calls laid out for you; so many a day, so many times a year, and you have to write reports on what happened and have your results analysed and then either commended or condemned. In the hotel, you will probably have to do all this for yourself; the security of supervision as well as the distaste of a ruling hand are missing. The targets are very often up to you, as are the number of calls you make over any given period. It is usually very easy to make acceptable excuses for why you failed: 'he said the price was too high', 'he said his numbers had gone up', or 'his boss has made other arrangements'. So it is the decision to pick up the telephone and try again for the tenth time when you have already been turned down nine times that separates the men from the boys.

Persistence produces the finest results and has its own special additional reward. For the man who is going to try to take the business from you when you have finally obtained it from a difficult client is going to have to do all the work you have done already. The client who is difficult to move to you, is difficult to move from you so long as you keep him happy. He won't flit round like a butterfly. If the first party is difficult to get, the second will be easier, and as time goes by it can become a matter of course that the client will use you.

Persistence is a gut reaction; the determination of the cross-country runner to run harder when all he wants to do with every aching muscle is to collapse, comes from willpower. A salesman needs willpower but he also needs what I can only describe as lateral thinking. For example, I was once trying to persuade a motor car manufacturer to launch his new product in my ballroom instead of choosing one of the great luxury hotels. The client was prepared to give it consideration, but he pointed out that it was impossible to get the car into the ballroom in the first place; it wouldn't go through the doors. At that point it is normal to shrug one's shoulders and hope for better luck next time; we knocked the wall down! The profits from the party were going to be far greater than the cost of knocking down the wall and widening the entrance, and we had the additional advantage of being able to get larger exhibits into the room in future, so there was every justification for the alteration. But the solution to the client's problem was an example of lateral thinking, in that it was way outside the normal behaviour patterns of a hotel.

There should be a sign up in every manager's office reading, 'Don't tell me why it can't be done. Tell me how to do it!' – because there is a solution to almost every problem if you try hard enough to find it. Recently a young manager was telling me that he had been asked by an Arab organiser to provide a menu which included whole stuffed lamb; so he had spent a lot of time working out exactly what size lamb he could get into the ovens. He had not tried to get the client to have *Piccata de Veau au Marsala* instead because it was a more normal banqueting dish. He had gone all out to give the client what he wanted. Examples abound of salesmen finding solutions to problems, but it can only happen if there is both determination and positive thinking.

It is often said of successful salesmen that they are born salesmen, but selling is a skill that can be taught and it does not fit only the naturally outgoing personality. Many excellent salesmen are basically shy people who have over-come their reticence. Nevertheless the effects of the original personality are there beneath the surface. It is perhaps the most contentious point salesmen ever discuss; the question of whether you could ascribe certain personality traits to particular individual clients within a short time of meeting them. I have said you cannot sum them up completely, but can you get clues? There is a school of psychiatrists who say you can; they divide people into introverts and extroverts: not wildly introverted because such people are mad, and not wildly extroverted for the same reason. But the doctors say that people tend towards extroversion or introversion. Those tendencies are not to be consi-dered as criticism in any way; it seems to me that an extrovert might be the first person into a burning building to help in the rescue, but the introvert would have checked to see the cigarette was extinguished in the beginning! The theory is that extroverts tend to be active, sociable and impulsive. Intro-verts tend to be less active, less sociable, and cautious. As an extrovert, I said to the scientist who was explaining this to me, 'I agree active and sociable, but why impulsive? What about that sound, thoughtful, executive judgement all the extroverts manage?' He patiently explained that the traits go together, whether we like it or not, and, of course, he is right. You can train yourself to be less impulsive, but the tendency to be so remains with you always.

Now you can see that the extrovert has some considerable natural advan-tage as a salesman. Being active, he will enjoy bustling round to see clients, and being sociable he will enjoy meeting new people. Being impulsive, he will tend to act without sufficient forethought in the attempt to get the business; but you can watch that problem. The introvert will find meeting strangers a little more difficult but he has the advantage that he will think very carefully before committing the company to something that cannot be done properly. It seems to me that extroverts are more normally cut out to be salesmen and introverts to be buyers, but there are plenty of exceptions in each case.

The doctors add a new dimension, however, to this theory. They have identified that extroverts and introverts have different décor and sartorial preferences. Extroverts prefer plain colours and large patterns, and introverts prefer small patterns. On the face of it that sounds crazy; that we should select patterns because of our innate personalities. But if you consider yourself an extrovert, do you often wear patterned socks? If you consider yourself an introvert, do you like large patterns? I can only tell you that experience does bear out this apparently fantastic idea. You see a client for the first time and he is wearing a small-patterned tie, and much more often than not you find you are dealing with an introvert. Don't take my word for it; try it out for yourself.

We must learn to recognise our own strengths and weaknesses. A sales-man who is not very sociable will take a dislike to a client who always wants to spend a lot of time socialising, unless he recognises the reason for the difference in approach. The trait of impulsiveness or caution must be watched; but the effect on the client of his own personality traits can also give us useful leads. For example, your banqueting room is going to appeal to one group or the other. You cannot have an ornate Victorian room which appeals to extroverts unless the décor is very bold; modern, clean architectural lines are not going to appeal to introverts except on hygienic grounds. You should, therefore, be on your guard for customer resistance to the banqueting room when you show it to the 'wrong' personality. The way to deal with this is to observe the customer carefully for facial reaction. If you are satisfied that the room does not appeal, the correct approach is, 'Of course, Mr Gibbons, this room doesn't appeal to everybody, but it is a great attraction to the Ladies/it doesn't overpower the appeal of your product displays/it is very popular with the older/younger generation' (selecting the age span which fits the majority of his guests) and so on.

Another hint that accurate analysis of extroversion/introversion gives you, comes at the point when you ask for the business. If the answer is effectively 'I'll have to give it some thought', your judgement of the import of that remark depends on your assessment of the client's personality. Thus an introvert who is cautious will say it because it is part of his normal make-up; you should accept the inevitable and leave him to think. The correct reaction is to ask, 'When would you like to reach a decision?' If an extrovert says it, however, this is the impulsive man, and he should have made up his mind without needing more time to think. When he asks for more time, therefore, it is far more likely that he is stalling; having accepted your hospitality he does not want to turn you down, but that is his future intention. Such a remark from an extrovert is a signal to redouble your efforts to solve his problems and resolve his doubts.

The professional salesman needs sensitivity, but not to be over-sensitive, that is to say to be easily hurt by a harsh word; that kind of personality will never make a good salesman. He must be sensitive in the way that enables him to feel a mood or an attitude in others. He must constantly be on the look-out for the sales presentation starting to go aground or heading for the rocks. Just as a piano-tuner can hear a key slightly off pitch, the good salesman has an ear and almost an early warning system for when things are likely to go wrong in the next few minutes. A salesman can deal with objections; a good salesman will anticipate the answers to the objections before they emerge. A good professional salesman will voice the objections, together with the answer, before the client does.

Imagine that the client with the large top table is looking at the ballroom you want to sell for the function. There is a silence, or a loss of concentration by the client on what you are saying. He is looking at the obvious place for setting up the top table. The correct procedure is to pause yourself, and then say something like, 'I've been thinking about your top table. What would really look excellent in this room would be a horseshoe top table. It would give your V.I.P.'s that much more room.' If the client's face clears, if he comes back to you mentally and is pleased with the suggestion, you have anticipated his worry accurately. If not, you must prise it out of him.

Why not wait for the complaint? Because, before it is voiced, the client is saying to himself, 'I don't like this room because . . . and I wonder whether another hotel has a better one'. You must keep the client on the main track and not heading for a dead-end siding culminating in a rival hotel. Supposing the client was perfectly happy with the top table and had something else entirely on his mind? Then you weren't attuned to the client's thinking, and you need to be. It takes time to master this particular skill, but it is part of the professional salesman's weaponry.

Another hidden weapon the good salesman needs is a capacity for mental arithmetic. I consider myself fortunate to have been brought up in a world where calculating machines didn't exist, because in those days mental arithmetic was drummed into us. Nowadays it is possible for a machine to do the calculating much faster and with absolute accuracy. For a salesman, what is so bad about that? Quite simply that the act of using the calculator informs the client that you are going to work out the costs in detail.

Let us consider an example; the client has a budget of £2,000 for the function and he has told you what items he would like it to include. What sort of menu are you able to offer, he asks. A lot of hoteliers would show the client a selection of sample menus, starting from their minimum price. Yet what the budget provides is a menu at a specific price; i.e. when you have allowed for the cost of the other items which must be included in the budget – cocktails, wine, liqueurs, menu printing and so on – what remains can be spent on the menu. So you tick off in your mind the approximate cost of each item – £1.50 for cocktails, £1 for wine, 60p for a liqueur or whatever – multiply by the expected number of guests, subtract the total from £2,000, divide the answer by the number of guests and that is the figure the client can afford for the menu. Let us assume that your minimum price for a four-course dinner is £5.00 and the budget allows for £7.00; the difference would be lost to the hotel if the client chooses a minimum-priced menu.

Why not work it all out on paper in front of the client? Because you want him to select a splendid menu rather than an indifferent one, on the basis that he can afford it and will be more likely to enjoy it. Once he has selected the dishes, the cost will not worry him, but if you talk about a £7.00 menu at the start, he will be likely to consider lowering his budget because he can do the job more cheaply than he had thought. Why not just let him buy what he wants? Because when it comes to the crunch, the professional salesman works for the hotel company, its shareholders and staff rather than for anybody else.

This integrity towards the interests of the hotel should not, however, mean sacrificing the interests of the client. A salesman guards his client's interests fiercely, as we have seen, in a constant attempt to get the client to come back again and again. The client sets the budget; the salesman tries to ensure that the total budget is spent and not more.

Quite obviously one of the major weapons a salesman uses is language, and command of the language is extremely important. A good salesman needs the largest possible vocabulary because he is communicating ideas, and the main danger is to fail to convey his meaning accurately. The nuances of the English language enable you to put over a concept with complete precision so long as you have the vocabulary: and there is no substitute for it. No amount of charm or elegance really makes up for being at a loss for the right words. To take a crude example, consider the difference between, 'What do you want?' and 'What would you like?' Four small, simple words, but a great difference in tone.

It is attention to the detail of words which again emphasizes the importance of detail itself in successful selling. In one of the earliest books on hotel sales promotion, Coffman's *Profits Through Promotion*, he mentions a saying of Benjamin Franklin's, 'Perfection is made up of little things, but perfection is not a little thing'. After 200 years, that remains as true as the day it was first said. A good salesman pays attention to every minute detail. Not without the occasional grumble, because poring over nitty-gritty detail is not the most exciting of activities, but doggedly persevering because if you get every detail right, the result is going to be a resounding success. On those rare occasions when a hotel actually books two parties into the same room, one wonders whether there has been any attention to detail whatsoever!

I would also put taste and showmanship high on the list of the attributes of a good hotel salesman. Taste is a difficult virtue to acquire, partly because it involves considering things important which you may not personally believe to be so. Does it really matter if a napkin is folded slightly off centre, or if a single flower in the top table display has dropped? For people with taste, every detail is important, for the possession of taste implies a close attention to the minutiae of gracious living. It is the ability to show clients a way of life which is a little more elegant than their own, a little more exciting than they normally enjoy, which is part of the stock-in-trade of the good hotelier, and that includes the good hotel salesman.

The creativity of producing something special for the client was one of the traditions of great hoteliers like César Ritz, and this has come down to us as

168

valid today as it was at the turn of the century. A good deal of expertise still taught in the hotel industry has to do with the acquisition of taste, and it runs like the royal purple through all we set out to achieve. It was said that Ritz could tell if the bottom sheet on a bed was creased without lifting the coverlet, which is no mean trick if you can do it: the point that this emphasizes is that no detail is too insignificant to be done perfectly, or to be supervised properly.

Finally, the professional hotel salesman must have the interests of his clients at heart. To gain their confidence and to ensure that they always come back to you, they must trust you always to look after them with complete honesty. Many years ago I was trying to get a soap company to give me the Chairman's dinner. We were already looking after the monthly meetings, but the Chairman's dinner was a very expensive affair and money was no object. The company had been using an excellent hotel with a very elegant banqueting room. The organiser explained to me very kindly that it was really no contest because the other hotel provided excellent service, splendid cooking and a beautiful room. Nevertheless we looked after that Chairman's dinner for a number of years thereafter. It so happened that, on the last occasion the company used that excellent hotel, the Chairman settled down to enjoy his cigar after a fine dinner in those lovely surroundings. Looking round the room, he happened to notice a wine waiter decanting liqueurs into ginger ale bottles and putting them into his back pocket. At that point the Chairman, who knew he was going to be charged for the liqueur involved, lost interest in that fine hotel. He instructed his organiser to move the function to me in future, because he knew there would be no shenanigans if he came to my hotel.

Now that simply shows the ill effects of downright crude dishonesty. But you don't have to be actually dishonest to lose customers. Remember the client with the German menu we discussed in the first chapter. If you don't tell the client the absolute truth, you can be pretty sure that somebody else will come along to fill the gap in the client's knowledge for you!

13

And Now?

If you carry out the recommendations in this book, you are going to invest a great deal of extra time and effort in getting banqueting business. It will be a sound investment, because you will achieve greater turnover and profit, but there is a way of doubling, trebling and quadrupling that profit into infinity; with a lot of functions, you can get the business year after year. Some of the banquets I sold into the new Europa Hotel in the early 1960s are still there fifteen years later. That business was at other hotels before I got it, and it is a severe criticism of the competence of those hotels that seldom was any effort made to take the business away from me again.

A big account is never yours by right, no matter how hard you work to keep the client happy. I looked after parts of the main sales conference for a frozen food manufacturer for 20 years from 1955, but never waited for them to contact me. First of all, it is impolite for the customer to chase the supplier, and secondly I didn't want to take any risk that the client had decided – even at very long last – to make a change without my knowledge.

It is amazing how even a small error can sour a relationship after many years. On one occasion I was trying to get a big pharmaceutical company to give me their banqueting business. They were using a large railway hotel at the time and the best I had to offer was a very small hotel with limited facilities. I was not very surprised that the client was resisting my efforts on the perfectly logical grounds that he was at a better hotel, perfectly satisfied and had been there for years. Nevertheless, we did get the business and what happened was this. One day the organiser had taken his wife shopping in the area of the railway hotel and dropped in afterwards for a cup of tea. He was sitting in the lounge, and the manager noticed him there. So he came over to the client, chatted briefly about the reason for his presence and then went away, leaving the client *to pay for his own tea*. The client had given the hotel many thousands of pounds' worth of business and he strongly resented the fact that the hotel manager would not even offer him a free cup of tea. You might think that unjustified, but many people cannot personally afford the hotels they use for their companies, and it was only a modest snack. So he left in a fury and brought the business to me. Not only was the business lost on such a small point, but at no time in the future did the railway hotel ever try to get the business back. They apparently never even noticed that it had gone. This was many years ago, but it taught me a very good lesson.

There are a number of fallacies about repeat business. The idea, for example, that if the job is done well, the client will automatically return. That should be true, but it is not, because the job might not have been done as well as you imagined. Also the desire on the part of a client for change is often strong; a new organiser might take over and be a new broom. There are many other reasons too. There are those who believe that the client should be a supplicant, asking the hotel for the space, rather than the hotel asking the client for the business. I don't think we need to discuss that if you have reached this point! And the idea that there are so many other important things to do; we are prepared to take the risk that the client might leave while we finish preparing the statistics on ice-cream consumption, or something equally unimportant, but which is less hard work emotionally than selling.

The correct analogy is with a garden; it is beautiful and productive as long as you work to keep it that way. Neglect it – even for one year – and it will revert to a wilderness which will be twice as difficult to reclaim.

So how do we keep the customers coming back for more? Well, let us ask another question; why don't they come back? Perhaps the most important reason is that they think they have been cheated in some way; particularly that they have been overcharged for drinks. The sad thing is that there are too many occasions in our industry when they have. It is an area of petty pilferage which management has great difficulty in suppressing. Even management itself is on occasions not above this practice. It is theft, and if *any* member of the staff steals and the client is charged for the consumption, then the culprit, if caught, should be prosecuted. We would want that to happen if we were deliberately shortchanged by a shop. If we found it occurring, the very least that would happen is that we would take our business elsewhere. The best safeguards for the hotel are to keep to the client's budget – as previously agreed – and to ensure that everybody knows that petty larceny is not company policy; that the client is not fair game.

Some clients do leave because they want a change. They get tired of the same old thing. The exception to the rule is when an event becomes a tradition: one would hardly stop playing test matches at Lords, move Henley into the English Channel, or have Buckingham Palace garden parties at Sandringham. The core of tradition is familiarity and there are short cuts to achieving this situation at an hotel. The client wants to be at home, recognised and welcome. Now the manager may recognise him and greet him, 'Good evening Mr Coxwell. Is everything to your liking?' But do the other staff? Does the wine waiter come up to him and say, 'I'm Harry Smith, the Head Wine Waiter, Mr Coxwell. Is there anything special your Chairman likes?' Or the cloakroom attendant, 'Good evening, Mr Coxwell. I hope it's a lovely evening'. Everybody can make the organiser feel that he has been at the hotel for ever, *if* they are properly briefed. And first-name terms between manager and client help to strengthen this sense of belonging.

The desire for change is perfectly natural after a period of time, but it is a hard pill to swallow that the devil a client doesn't know is considered by him to be better than the one – you – that he does know. That is a pretty severe criticism of the standards you set. To try a new staff, a new chef, a brigade of waiters who don't know the function, and all this after being looked after by you; a pretty severe criticism indeed. It should be quite easy to satisfy the desire for change under those circumstances if you recognise the possibility, offer alternative themes – Victorian, Italian, Hawaiian or whatever. You can create special effects with the menu, ring the changes on menu design, and take advantage of the chapter on creative banqueting. The client may not want to change, he may be happy to stay doing what he did last year, and if that is the case all is well. But don't fail to check that seven-year itch, which in our industry is more likely to come after three years.

Important as organisers are, they would be the first to admit that there are other V.I.P.s. If those ladies and gentlemen are unhappy, you can also lose repeat business. We all know that, and the attention paid to the top table is one of the traditions in our industry which is carefully maintained. The mistake to avoid is failing to identify exactly who are the V.I.P.s; all of them. Don't miss one.

We all have fond memories of hotels. I remember a marvellous steak I was served at an hotel in the North on the night before I got married; the poached egg on smoked haddock they served for breakfast at a seaside hotel when I was a child, and a superb mushroom soup, home-made at a restaurant outside Carlisle. I never went back to any of them; nobody ever asked me to. That's one of the key reasons why business is lost. You know when to ask for it – when the client is starting to think about the function, about a month before he comes to his final decision. Then you are not bothering him, but you are showing your continued interest and your efficiency. In a busy year, you have the time and the careful records to contact him. That is impressive; that shows organisation. It is not the easiest of systems.

I knew a manager once who contacted everybody three months before the date of the function. So if it had been held in December last year, he contacted them in September this year. All he had to do was get out last year's banqueting book and on September 1st he would start to ring all the previous December's parties. What could be simpler for the manager to organise? The only problem was that many of the clients had already made their decisions, and for some it was still too early. The clients were supposed to realise that their erratic decision-making was inconvenient to the hotel, and would they please decide three months in advance in future! Clients are not like that and we must fit in with their pattern of decision-making, not vice versa.

We fail to get repeat business because we win arguments. If a client has a complaint – and things go wrong in the best-organised hotels – we put up a tremendous defence of our young (the staff) and fight off the attacker. It is said that the British lose every battle except the last one. Hotels can win all those battles with the client on complaints; but if they lose the final battle of whether he will come back, they might just as well not have won the early ones. The client is always right: what an old cliché, but then a cliché is often an eternal verity. It is sometimes difficult to find a reason for the client being right because there are many occasions when he is absolutely wrong. On such occasions you must fall back on, 'I'm so sorry I didn't make that clear. How foolish of me'. Or , 'Well, of course. Now I come to think of it, I should certainly have told you about that in advance.' Very useful when the client is complaining that the hotel didn't stock Peruvian Panatellas! The client is never wrong and if he is on the attack, you are retreating, full of apologies, if you want to retain the business. 'But it's so unfair,' the amateurs moan. It is also unfair when you get far more than your share of the available business, and far more functions than the quality of your product justifies. That sort of unfairness is perfectly acceptable to us all, so the other variety must be as well.

How do you deal with complaints? First of all, you listen. Never interrupt a client who is complaining. Let him talk himself out, no matter how long it takes, just like a storm blowing itself out. Second, take notes. That proves to the client that you are taking him seriously and that you intend to do something about it. It also helps you to prepare the remarks you are going to make when you do finally get a chance to speak. Third, apologise. Either because you were wrong, or make up some explanation which justifies your saying you were wrong. Fourth, tell the client what you are going to do about his complaint. And then do it as quickly as is humanly possible. A complaint properly handled can often bind the customer even more closely to the hotel, because he will inevitably contrast your reaction to those of a less professional management. Everybody makes mistakes, and the client will make allowances *as long* as you deal with the complaint correctly.

Lastly, we lose business because we get slack. We make a tremendous effort to get the business, we make another to get it back again the following year; but as time goes by, we get complacent. We start to take Mr Coxwell for granted. If there is a heavy banqueting week, then we feel that at least we can relax when we get to Mr Coxwell's dinner. That party always comes back, and so we slacken just a little and then a little more, and Mr Coxwell notices and starts to think that perhaps the time has come to make a change. It is indeed very hard to keep up the energy and enthusiasm when the sixth time comes round, but if you only consider all the difficulties you are going to have replacing Mr Coxwell's business, you might make that little extra effort just to save yourself the bother of finding a new client for that night.

This book should, ideally, be thought of as no more than an introduction to what it takes to get more banquets, to fill those empty dates, to make those extra profits. Now all you have to do is carry on learning, read more books and add to your knowledge of creative banqueting, effective advertising, letter writing, more fluent selling on a telephone; plus a greater understanding of the needs of the client. I spent over twenty years at it and I'm sure I didn't learn it all. That is, in fact, the fascination of selling; you never do learn it all, just as there are chess variations Messrs Korchnoi and Karpov have yet to discover, new mountains to climb, new answers to find. I can only hope that you get as much enjoyment out of it as I did, meet just as many fascinating people, and watch just as many guests enjoying themselves that little bit more because *they* bought a banquet from *you*.

Index

INTERNATIONAL HOTEL AND CATERING
MANAGEMENT CONSULTANT

Alfred Motson F.H.C.I.M.A., F.C.F.A.
34 BADINGHAM DRIVE, FETCHAM PARK,
SURREY KT22 9EU
TEL: LEATHERHEAD (53) 75146